The Other Child
A Parent's Guide

Rachel A. Ormsby

The Other Child: A Parent's Guide

ISBN-13: 978-1544284651 (TheOtherChildNB)

ISBN-10: 1544284659

A CreateSpace ISBN.

Printed in the United States of America

DEDICATION

This book is dedicated to Kate because her battle was just as hard as Nathan's.

A child who is integrated into caring for a sick sibling learns so many things that will benefit them throughout their lives. Love for the sick sibling may be the most important.

ACKNOWLEDGEMENTS

Thank you to my daughter Kate for being such a strong powerful influence in my life and sticking with me through this process.

Thank you to my husband Scott for supporting Kate and myself.

Thank you to my cousin Julie, who told me one day that she had been diagnosed with Chronic Myelogenous Leukemia (CML), but she would be ok and it would just be a new life change. She then told me that she was going to keep her three boys lives "normal" through the process. At that moment, this subject got a voice. I thank her for being tolerant during my tirade to her about not making the same mistakes that I have made.

Thank you to Dr. Sonata Jodele for being a driving force to help families fighting these diseases and me to write books.

INTRODUCTION

In May 2013, my husband and I self-published the book "…Learning to Dance in the Rain: A Parent's Guide to Neuroblastoma Diagnosis, Treatment and Beyond". Writing the book about our son's trip through cancer was difficult, heart-wrenching and something I never planned to do. My husband, Nathan's doctor, friends and God pushed me through it. The final product is not our memoirs but a guide to parents who just entered the world of pediatric cancer. It explains all the lessons we learned about treatments, scans and just surviving. The 16 months it took to finish the book were cathartic, but it was very difficult to relive those long years. However, I was compelled because I felt we had done the absolute best for Nathan and we have our son still with us to prove it.

Now it is time to talk about our other child, Kate.

I have had the idea to write this book for several years. While the advice and lessons I will talk about may now appear obvious; sometimes stating the obvious has the best results. What we learned over the years of dealing with our son's cancer is that taking care of children who are not sick is just as important as taking care of children who are sick.

When Nathan was diagnosed with stage IV Neuroblastoma Scott and I attacked it head on. We researched what we needed to do for him. We talked to doctors, nurses and hospitals. We reached out to other families to find the best way to help him get through and survive this disease. It never occurred to us that we should use that same diligence to find the best way to care for our daughter during her journey through Nathan's disease. We went about life with her as if nothing had happened to her at all. Somehow, we developed a very interesting perspective that her life would be fine on the periphery of Nathan's disease. We were certain it would be better for her there. In hindsight, I think this perspective was very wrong.

At the time, my reasoning seemed very sound and logical. "I want her to have a normal life," "I don't want to expose her to the hospital," "She will be bored at the hospital," "I just don't have the energy to handle her too" and so on. The biggest and most harmful excuse was "I need to focus on our son now, later I will fix any hurt or problems we caused our daughter." I now know that ALL of these statements are false and dangerous.

Our philosophy as a family was to keep our daughter away from cancer and the hospital as much as possible. We went to great lengths to accomplish this and now, ten years later, our daughter has several things she deals with.

> First, she thinks the hospital is some place "really awesome" and fun, since her brother and mom spent so much time there alone, without her. When mom was home, dad was at the hospital.
> Second, she is uniquely aware that her life was not normal but, it never was going to be. As soon as cancer entered our family, ALL our lives were changed, including hers. In our misplaced desire to keep her out of cancer, she had an even more "not normal" childhood. We did not allow her to participate in our new world and inadvertently made her feel like an outsider.
> Third, taking care of our daughter would not have required more energy. It would most definitely have given more energy than it took. It could have centered our lives on living and dancing, not on problems, death and cancer. Kate energized any room she entered.
> Finally, trying to get things back to the way they were before cancer cannot happen. With constant love, an incredible amount of patience and an infinite supply of understanding and attention from her family, we believe, Kate now realizes how much we care for her. She is finding her way through life with some baggage related to Nathan's cancer, but with the solid foundation of a family who adores her and always has.

We are encouraging our daughter to see things differently by having very raw, safe, open conversations with her. We are trying to overcome the hurt we have caused by showing and telling her what she means to us and how she fits into our family. Over the years, we found help when we introduced Kate to the most wonderful Christian counselors. We believe that if she puts Christ into her life, then she will receive someone who loves her unconditionally. The counselors also helped us see things from Kate's point of view and helped us get some idea of what we need to do to repair the pain and get rid of some of the baggage she carries. I am more intentional to tell her daily how much I adore her and why. The hurt to Kate's self-esteem is deep and unfair to her. I wish that I could have known how to do this differently. When we were just starting, I wish I had someone tell me the falsehoods in my assumptions and decisions before we were so deep into the battle with cancer.

In this book, I will share those things I wish I had known at the beginning. I will address each of our misconceptions and give some examples of how we could have done this in a way to help our daughter to be stronger and a more loving, empathetic, caring person.

As I prepared to write this book, I mentioned this topic to several friends. The response I received was amazing and very supportive. The thing I learned most from the comments from friends is that my rationale was not unique. Many families facing similar types of hardships, not all cancer but all equally overwhelming, choose the same approach we did. For example, my friend Pam responded with:

> *"I've thought about this topic many times. My sister was very sick (but not cancer) when we were young. I acclimated. I learned that I was not as important and that was okay. My friends lost their son to brain cancer but loved each other and their daughter well. My other friend who lost her son to cancer last year I watched tearfully as her family has completely fallen apart. She and her husband divorced and her other two sons are distant and have turned to drugs to ease their pain."*

And her email signature verse is very appropriate:

> *"So, do not fear, for I am with you; do not be dismayed, for I am your God. I will strengthen you and help you; I will uphold you with my righteous right hand." Isaiah 41:10*

As I look back at our battle with cancer I realize that God gave us the most precious gift of our daughter prior to our son getting sick. He gave us someone who would make the hardships easier by giving us laughter, joy and an outlet from the world of cancer. However, instead of embracing Kate for the gift she was, we tried to protect her. We put her on a pedestal to be adored and loved but excluded her as a full participant in our family. Now we are together making amends and moving forward. She is fully integrated into our insanely busy lives and seems to love each moment of it. In fact, recently when Nathan was hospitalized for a collapsed lung Kate spent a lot of hours at the hospital with him. Her response was very telling of her perspective "Mom, you spent 10 years doing this!? How boring."

In the pages that follow I will try to explain what we learned through our wonderful daughter Kate. She knows I am writing this book and is being the best resource any mother could have. I pray that through these pages other children will be found and loved.

Table of Contents

CHAPTER 1. SURVIVOR STORY

Each summer our family attends the Children's Neuroblastoma Cancer Foundation's (CNCF) parent conference in Chicago. This conference is presented by a mother who lost her son, Nick, to Neuroblastoma. She created CNCF with two objectives: to raise money to fund a cure for Neuroblastoma and to educate parents about their treatment options. Each year she gathers medical experts to present the current state of research on the disease. Each afternoon she has Neuroblastoma survivors speak to the audience. These survivors are true superstars at the conference.

Survivor stories generally follow the same flow. The survivor tells how they were diagnosed at an early age, such that they do not remember it. They tell the audience the stories that were told to them by parents and friends who lived through it with them. Then they tell about the early days they do remember. They discuss the pain. They tell the weird side effects or "late effects" they are living with. Many times, they say how everything tastes weird. They tell how school was so very difficult due to "chemo-fog", a well-documented side effect of chemotherapy where their brains feel like they are always cloudy such that it is difficult to focus on details. They tell about the physical limitations such as hearing loss, small stature and pain. They show wonderful and horrible photos of their lives.

The parents hang on to every word these survivors speak. They pray that their child will someday be able to tell a story like this and yet they know in their minds, if not their hearts, that their child who is fighting neuroblastoma only has a 50-50 chance to survive at all. When I listen to the stories, I feel that there is absolutely no reason the person talking to us should have defeated this disease and yet they did. These survivor stories fill the room with hope where many parents feel their children have absolutely no chance to survive. These stories are those gems in a weekend of horrible facts and limited advances in treatment.

Then came this one survivor a few years ago. I apologize for not remembering his name or his specific background to give him full credit for affecting my life so profoundly. This man, in his 30's, got up and told the audience something that he hoped would help them. He did not tell a story that sounded like so many others. He had a warning for parents. He started by telling this audience that, when it came to his family, it did not matter if he lived or died from neuroblastoma. His family was destroyed either way. Here he was; he survived and yet his family had not. His parents had divorced and his siblings had some serious issues. One is suffering from PTSD, while his other sister is the strongest person you will ever meet. This survivor was telling these exhausted parents there was something even worse than losing their child. He was telling them that they could lose their child that was fighting cancer and they could lose everything else in their lives.

His presentation started in the same way as so many others. He was a toddler when diagnosed with neuroblastoma. The disease had spread from his adrenal gland to his skeleton. He was riddled with it. He was given a 5% chance of survival. He told us that his mom and dad "did their best" for him. He made the point that they did care for him, but they forgot to care for themselves and his sisters. Like so many families and mothers like me, his mother had moments where she needed to make horrible decisions. She needed to choose between her child who is fighting cancer and her children who were watching her child fight cancer. These decisions seem so small and so easy to pick initially, but they stack up on top of each other. The idea that the "cancer" decisions are independent of the rest of the family is the place I must admit, I also failed my family.

As I listened to him, it was easy to imagine him talking about me and my family. He mentioned his sister who was the best most adjusted woman he knows. Then he talked of his other sister who is angry at everything. She cannot cope with anything going wrong. She takes all failures personally and her successes do not appear to mean anything anyway. He spoke how his sister took every comment, every event, as a personal attack and every compliment as insincere. The inadvertent comments about "keep things clean so you don't get your brother sick" or "cover your mouth when you are going to cough, you don't want to send your brother to the hospital" resonated in her.

There are so many trivial things we can say that can hurt to the core a person who is too young to understand. Can you imagine how it would feel for a small child to know that something they do may kill their brother? Some children take these as challenges head on, but others cannot and do not. They ingest the information as if it is completely true and the thought of hurting someone that badly cuts them deeply.

This man's survivor talk planted in me the seed to fix things with my own daughter. We took some time to look at everything we had done during our son's treatment from the eyes of our daughter. She feels everything deeply and personally. From the perspective of this survivor, we could see our mistakes or missteps and the choices we could have made differently. We looked at all the families we had met in our journey. We started to realize that there was a different way to walk our path than the way we chose.

After the survivor talked, we had another talk from Dr. Hillary Van Horn-Glatin. She is a Behavioral Medicine Psychologist at Kaiser Permanente in Sacramento, CA. She presented the talk "The Emotional Strains of Childhood Cancer". Her talk was about siblings and family members contracting Post Traumatic Stress Disorder (PTSD) as part of the treatment process of a family member. Her talk can be seen at: https://www.youtube.com/watch?v=boGmVhYM0Yk.

These two talks together put several things together in my mind. I could relate these talks to my family and our journey and how we treated our daughter. We had the "best of intentions" towards her and caring for her, but we gave her what we wanted her to have instead of what was best for her. We gave her a life outside of cancer when an integrated life in the world of cancer would have been a better choice for her.

During our time of cancer treatment, our daughter has had her own issues. She has found how to get our attention and not in the best ways possible. She has adapted to her life but not as we wanted. We went through cancer treatment for our son saying that when cancer treatment was over, we could put all our focus on her. Well, cancer treatment took 10 years. That is a long time to push off the needs of a child.

We believe that there is a way to raise the healthy child (or children) during treatment for cancer of your sick child. You do not need to sacrifice the care of one child for the care of the other child. My family was fortunate that we noticed things going awry and took steps to improve them. We have also been blessed that our son survived his battle with cancer and still has a whole family together to spend his life with.

Now, I have God tapping me on the back of my head telling me that I need to share what we have learned so that other families who are battling any long-term issue can have a different plan and will care for all their family and themselves.

CHAPTER 2. OUR LIVES CHANGED FOREVER

Let us start our story with a little history. My husband, Scott and I have always wanted several children. Each of us grew up with multiple siblings and something about learning to thrive through these relationships has made us the people we are today. We wanted our children to share in the trials and tribulations of being one child of many. Scott and I decided to have children several years after we were married when we were stable enough that we could give them the attention we wanted for them. Having children was not easy or straight forward for us. It took us seven years to finally have our son, Nathan. The pregnancy with Nathan was filled with complications and the delivery almost ended my life. My doctor, our families, Scott and I agreed that I should not give birth to another child. Having one child at the age of 37 was difficult, having a second when I would be even older, would be dangerous. We would find another way to have the family we wanted. It took us seven years to have our first child, it took another two and one-half years to get our second. Kate entered our lives to the adoring hands of Scott and Nathan when she was just 20 minutes old.

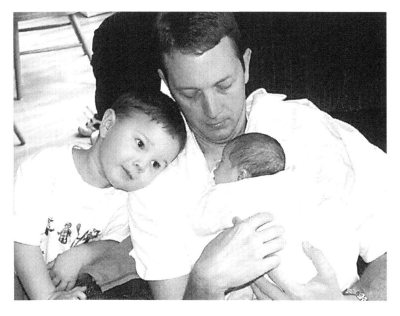

Figure 1 - Kate and her boys, Dad and Nathan

Kate quickly became the center of our universe. When Kate was a baby, she and Nathan shared a bedroom. Nathan would sit in his bed just watching her. He would talk with her and tell her all the big brother things he would do for her. Kate's first year was idyllic for our entire family. Scott's Air Force career was doing well and we were stationed at Wright Patterson Air Force Base. I had taken a year off from my engineering job and was to return as a part time employee when Kate was 18 months old. Then, she would go to the local Christian Academy for preschool with her brother. Nathan was growing and thriving while caring for his little sister. Scott and I had discussed adopting a third child but would wait until Kate was a bit older.

Our daughter Kate oozed personality. She was in charge of our family. She knew it and enjoyed it. We would spend our time watching her learn new skills while she was always in command of her audience. Nathan and Kate spent almost all their time together. Nathan would dote on her. He was mobile and could go and get anything she wanted. Kate stayed close to Nathan because he was also her translator. Kate was a late talker but an early climber. Scott and I had trouble understanding her, but not Nathan. When Kate got frustrated with trying to make her parents understand her, she would get Nathan. Tell him what to say. He would tell us. We would confirm with her that he was right, which he always was. Nathan and Kate were quite a pair.

Just after Kate's first birthday in July, Nathan started having pain in his right shin. We just had the shin and leg examined less than a month before, but the doctor and X-rays found nothing. When Nathan started having a high fever we consulted our "what to do when the child is sick" book, The Portable Pediatrician by Laura W. Nathanson. After three days with an unexplained fever, the books say to take the child to the doctor. There was no worry in me at this point, even though Scott was out of town and it was just me and the kids. I was pretty sure this was a set of ear infections. Kate also had a fever and was pulling on her ears. I expected a quick visit to the doctors that would include some antibiotics for the ear infections and we would continue along our lives.

Looking back on the events leading to Nathan's diagnosis, I can see several blessings showing how God was watching over us. Here was the first. The Air Force base pediatric clinic did not have an appointment for us. They were uncomfortable leaving Nathan's fever for another day, so they recommended we take both kids to the Emergency Room at the base hospital. The pediatric clinic would then follow up the next day when space was available on the schedule. This small detail that put us in the ER that day allowed us immediate access to the entire hospital staff and resources.

The Air Force hospital staff was fantastic. They immediately diagnosed Kate with an ear infection, gave her antibiotics and turned their attention to Nathan. Nathan did not have an ear infection. They started asking for other symptoms. I mentioned the weird leg pain, but those were all his symptoms: leg pain and a high fever. Kate was quickly fed up with the hospital, doctors and rules. She did like the nurses, many of them would spend time with her as I worked with the doctors and Nathan. The series of specialty doctors kept coming to evaluate Nathan, ending with Orthopedics. One-year old Kate was ready to leave well before the doctors were ready to let us go.

The Orthopedic doctor was straight and to the point. *"You will go to the Children's Hospital; they will put a needle in Nathan's right hip and take out a sample of the inflammation for testing. We will then find out what kind of infection is causing the fever and swelling in his right hip."* He informed us that shin pain was frequently an indication of inflammation in the hip. The doctor also recommended that we find a place for Kate to spend the night. Now, panic started settling in a bit. Hospitals are not the place you want to spend the night. A short visit was a lot less frightening than an expected overnight visit. We had some friends take Kate for the night while Nathan and I dealt with the children's hospital.

The next several days were hectic. Nathan and I were in and out of both the Children's hospital and the Air Force base hospital multiple times. Each time friends would take care of Kate. As things got more serious, Scott returned from his month-long business trip thanks to another Air Force pilot volunteering to take his place. Nathan was eventually admitted to the children's hospital for an undetermined amount of time with an undetermined problem. After 10 days of scans and tests, Nathan was diagnosed with stage IV Neuroblastoma on 8/8/06.

Figure 2 - Kate at the time of Nathan's diagnosis with Stage IV Neuroblastoma

While Nathan was in the hospital he endured enormous pain, but Kate had her own pain and anguish as she was shuffled around from friend to friend. Family members were brought in to care for her and love on her, while her parents and Nathan spent all their time in the hospital. Kate had moved from our family's center to its periphery because the cancer was now at our family's center.

With this new focus in our lives, we needed to make decisions for both of our children. The decisions for Nathan would be made with the help of the hospital staff of doctors, nurse, aides and child-life experts. The decisions for Kate would be ours with help from family and friends we could rally to help care for her.

Scott and I decided that we wanted to have Kate lead a normal life without having to deal with the world of cancer. We would keep her daily schedule the same as it was before cancer. We would have family come in and care for her. "How long could this take anyway?" At the beginning of the battle with Neuroblastoma we were so naive we felt it would only take a couple of months and then we would all go back to the way it was "before". After a couple of months of chemotherapy, scans, hospital visits and the like, Scott suggested that we send Kate to day care on the Air Force base. The completeness of my denial can be seen in my immediate negative reaction to his suggestion. Scott understood quicker than I did. This was going to be a long fight. If we wanted to keep Kate out of the battle, we needed to find a safe place for some consistency in her life. We still had several months before she would be old enough to attend the Christian Academy, and the base daycare would be just fine for now.

Over the next couple of years, we did our best to preserve Kate's life outside of the hospital and the world of cancer. At first glance, this may seem like a completely admirable way to care for Kate and Nathan. We would deal with cancer and the hospital when necessary. We would all live a perfectly normal "before" cancer kind of life when not dealing with cancer.

The big problem with this plan, quite simply, is that it just does not work. There is no dealing "with cancer and the hospital when necessary." When fighting such a horrible disease all family members are in the battle all the time. The "perfectly normal 'before' kind of life" no longer exists.

There is a funny thing about time, there is only one direction. Everyone only gets one chance to live each moment of their lives. It is not possible to put one life on hold until the issues of cancer are gone. Everyone in the family will experience the new world of cancer. It is not possible to exclude anyone and leave them out of it. If you try, there will be significant negative consequences, as we learned with our daughter Kate.

After Nathan was diagnosed with cancer, we had two options: we could either include Kate in our battle with cancer, or we could exclude her. There really is not a third option. We had a family of four. This family was going to deal with neuroblastoma. When a focus is so strong, there is no way to divide this family's attention between two completely opposite frames of reference, cancer and no cancer. So, our options were to either include Kate in our battle or exclude her from the family's biggest event.

We were under the false impression that Kate's life could be normal, where normal is how life was before cancer. It would be perfect if Kate did not have to suffer through cancer like the rest of her family would. In a perfect world, we would be able to let Kate live her life free from the effects of cancer in the family, while Scott and I helped Nathan battle his disease. We missed the fact that Kate's life had also changed. There was no going back to the prior normal for any of us. We, as a family, now had a new way of life. We as parents missed it.

Granted, Kate was very young at the time. I remember how she reacted to us being gone so frequently and I can now see how her behavior changed. By excluding her from cancer we taught her different ways to get our attention. Kate's personality was always sensitive. She was always very in tune with her family and how to get any reaction she wanted out of them. She had taken the previous year training us. Kate went from getting her brother to help her whenever she wanted it, to disliking having him around. When Nathan was around, his disease was always present. Since Nathan had such a horrible battle, it was difficult to separate the two lives (cancer and no cancer) when we were all together. The Doctors gave Nathan a very low chance to live 6 months from diagnosis. That needed to be our family's focus.

Kate's life was filled with waiting. Waiting for her parents to pick her up. Waiting for her brother to come home. Waiting for her family to return from wherever they were. To see the events from Kate's point of view, she must have been confused about her life. I was a stay at home mom and got to spend all my days with Kate doing mom and daughter stuff. Nathan attended the Christian Academy at our church and loved it. Suddenly I had my hands too full. Kate had love and attention from friends, aunts, uncles and grandparents that spent all their time just spoiling her rotten. She was doted on, cared for and loved beyond any normal child. However, it was not her mom, dad and brother doing the spoiling. She was missing her family. Her mother and brother were no longer there all day watching her and playing with her and giggling with her.

Figure 3 - Kate hanging out at home with her mother and brother

Kate's behavior changed during this early time during Nathan's treatment (called Frontline Therapy). She was always very attached to Mom, but the separation anxiety got very intense. If I dropped her off at daycare the screaming and tantrum lasted several hours after I left the building. She would take her frustration out on the children at the school. Biting and scratching were common occurrences. She would become more physical depending on her level of anxiety. Kate was a late talker and could not express her emotions in words, only in actions. The staff at the Christian Academy were excellent with her. They all understood what was happening in her life and took care of her. They would include her in everything they could. They would also allow her an escape when she needed it. They had a place she could go and calm down with no negative ramifications.

Kate decided the best way to protest what was happening in her life was to give up napping. Kate needed naps probably more than most children. However, during this time she absolutely refused to nap. This would facilitate worse moods and poorer behavior. Her behavior was not normally bad, but you could tell the level of stress the family was dealing with based upon the level of anger you could see in Kate.

In the evenings at home, I would take Kate for walks in her stroller. Kind neighbors would stop by and chat. Kate decided that she was not going to put up with yet another distraction. She was going to keep her mother all to herself. She would SCREAM until that kindly neighbor would leave. As soon as the neighbor walked away, the crying would stop. Once back at the house I would take her out of the stroller and put her on the floor to play. She would turn her back to me and play contentedly. When I tried to be involved in her play she would scream at me, then turn her back to me and again play contentedly. At the time, I decided not to fight her. I would lay down and fall asleep. In this simple act of falling asleep instead of playing with her, I allowed her to be in charge, not me. The battle for authority has continued to this day in basically the same way where the boundaries are always tested and pushed.

Kate's anger at her parents and battle for authority extended beyond us spending time with her. When she and I were together, she expected that everything that she wanted would be presented to her, immediately. She also expected that all my attention would be completely given to her whether she wanted it or not. She would ignore my hugs and efforts to play with her. When I finally gave up and went onto something else she was even madder. She acted as if my time was hers to do with what she wanted, even if it was to just ignore me. When things did not happen to her satisfaction her anger would flare and her temper would take over to the point where she no longer was able to control herself physically or verbally.

I realize that many children seem to have an issue with the word "no". Kids are fantastic when using the word, but few like hearing it back when asking a question. "May I have a cookie?", "Can we go to the amusement park?" and so on. If a parent says no to these things, frequently a child will be displeased with the parent, but in a few moments, will move on. Generally, kids realize when they are asking for something that is unlikely to happen they can handle the inevitable "no". Kate did not. To her, all things are possible right now. It got to the point where every conversation with her that did not go exactly as she expected it to, or wanted it to, ended in a very loud disagreement. It did not matter what she asked. "Can we go to the water park this weekend?" was a common question. Any answer other than "yes" would initiate an immediate negative response of yelling, kicking and a tantrum. Kate and I spent a few years where every conversation ended in her throwing some form of fit.

Kate pushed every conversation past a reasonable level of expectations. We had somehow convinced her that she did not need to accept her parents saying no to anything. I am still not exactly sure how we got to this point. I must assume that somehow this was a gauge for her. Let me explain. In Nathan's world, he could determine how sick he was by the level of rules that applied to him at any given time. Shooting Mom with Nerf darts from a Nerf gun was not tolerated. Mom always had something to say about getting hit by darts. A few times Nathan's situation seemed dire. He had shot me with his Nerf fun and there were no consequences to him. Nathan immediately went back to bed. He assumed he must be horribly sick if there was no punishment for shooting mom with darts. Maybe this behavior of Kate's was a similar gauge. You see, there was no reason for Nathan to shoot me with darts, and yet, on occasion, he would. And there was no reason Kate should expect us to go to a fancy water park every weekend, and yet she would ask, and then be upset when we said no.

We have asked ourselves; how in all of this did we teach Kate to act in this way? Kate was 1 year old when Nathan was diagnosed. She was the delight of everyone she came near. Nathan adored her and smiled from ear-to-ear when she was in the room. As the world of cancer encircled us, most everything was swept away but cancer. Our focus turned from normal activities to always being in crisis mode. In the middle of this crisis, Kate was no longer our focus. As I look back I have asked myself why wasn't she in the middle? She was one big ball of energy and excitement. Why was she not there fighting with us? Whenever she was around Nathan felt better. Whenever she was around Mom and Dad she smiled more. The more time she spent in the world of cancer, the less she acted out. Would it really be ok to have this wonderful bundle of personality battle with us? Was it acceptable to drag all the family members into this new reality of ours? I think it is.

So, why did we no include her more if it was so obvious? At the time, we felt it was unfair to Kate to have her go through the hospital boredom and monotony. Why would a little girl want to be at the hospital where there were germs and sick people? Why would she choose to deal with all the chaos the rest of us were working with? Why would she want to spend those beautiful summer days indoor? Looking back, the answer now seems clear and easy. She would want to do these things because it was her family at that hospital with the germs, indoors and therefore that is where she wanted to be as well. We felt we were completely separating her from cancer, when in fact we just separated her from us, not cancer. Cancer would always be part of her life since it was cancer that completely changed her world.

Our intentions sound perfectly appropriate for parents of a little girl. We wanted her to live the life the rest of us were no longer able to live. We wanted her to have a stress free, cancer free childhood where she would remember play dates at the houses of her friends, not in the play room at a hospital. We wanted her to have the life lost to us. These things were not important to her. She wanted to be part of the family fully and without limitations. What this girl wanted was to be in the trenches with us. A one or two-year-old little girl cannot sit her very stressed parents down and say "Hey Mom and Dad, include me more. I can handle it." But they can let their intentions and desires known in their own way. When Kate was included she was helpful, happy and accommodating. When she was excluded she was defiant, angry and difficult.

We eventually realized our mishandling of Kate and changed our behavior. We included her more in the care of Nathan. She would join us at doctor appointments that she hated. She would be allowed to watch us change Nathan's central line bandage that she thought was gross. She was allowed to listen to conversations about scheduling and time management for the week, which she thought was boring. We had her visit a professional to talk things out, where she colored instead of talked. But in each of these cases, she was right there the next time, sour face and all.

This book is intended to show the things we did right and wrong on how we handled our family while fighting cancer. We did several things correctly, but there are also several things I would do differently. Most importantly, I would be more inclusive with both of my children. It would be a change for better for the entire family.

In the rest of this book, I will go over those things we did and those things we should have done to make Kate's life better. I will elaborate in each instance why I think our actions were good or why they should have been different.

This book is organized as follows:

First, I go over some basics that we learned about dealing with cancer and a healthy child. This includes how a routine and journaling made a significant impact on keeping our lives less complicated. I discuss how open communication can make a huge positive impact on a family always in chaos. Then there are a few paragraphs about programs for kids that we have experienced and how the healthy children can be included.

Second, I will discuss each of the following excuses we used to justify our behavior and how we may have done things differently.

➤ "I want her to have a normal life"
➤ "I don't want to expose her to the hospital"
➤ "I just don't have the energy to handle her too"
➤ "I need to focus on our son now. Later I will fix any hurt we cause our daughter"

Third, in the book "...Learning to Dance in the Rain" I talk about Scott and my marriage and how cancer affected that relationship. It goes well with this discussion and has been included herein with only minor modifications.

Fourth, I have included a summary of Nathan's story. He is a large part of our path with Kate. An overview of his treatments will show why we were in chaos for so long.

Fifth and finally, a list of organizations and resources that helped us during our fight with cancer. Feel free to use these resources for your own battle.

At the end of each section is a place to write notes. Some place to put thoughts that can easily be lost with so much going on in a hectic life.

I am not a therapist trained in child behavior; I am just a mom who wishes I had handled my daughter with as much forethought as I handled my son. I pray that in these pages each family can find a routine and method that suits their family and how they can grow together instead of apart.

CHAPTER 3. DEALING WITH CANCER

During the first week after Nathan's diagnosis, Scott and I sat down with Nathan's doctor to have our Cancer 101 lesson so we could have a basic understanding of what was to come. In this talk, we learned why cancer was bad and that the body did not fight it because the body did not see cancer as foreign. We learned that remission was having less than a certain number of cancer cells in the body and that it really did not apply to this form of cancer. Neuroblastoma was so bad you either got completely rid of it, or you kept trying until you did. We learned the different types of blood cells and which ones we cared about and when. We learned the cycle of his chemotherapy, when Nathan would feel fine and when we needed to be extra careful.

Somewhere in these conversations with nurses and social workers, they told us that other children would be welcome in the hospital. No matter their age, siblings could take part of their brother's or sister's care. Most families, especially young families or families with single parents, cannot just exclude the siblings like we did. We saw some families bring their children in all the time and stay with the sibling in the hospital, while other families have children go spend time with grandparents. It was up to each family to make these decisions and the hospital would adapt.

I remember thinking that I did not want either of those options. If Kate went off to her grandparents' house I would not see her. I did not want to have her gone. I also remember not wanting to subject her to the hospital and all the stress and boredom she would see there. My logic was easy enough, I wanted Kate to live in her own home and see her parents and grow up normally.

There were several things we did not grasp our Cancer 101 lesson. First, Nathan and I would not be home very much over the next two years. Second, when I was home and Scott was in the hospital with Nathan, I was going to be tired. Third, I was teaching my daughter was that she was not first in my priorities. In fact, I was teaching her she was not on my priority list at all. I told myself several times that someday we would go back and fix whatever we were doing to Kate. Even this thinking shows that I knew at some level that what Kate was going through was not fair or necessary. But with no known solution, my tired brain chose what it considered the easier approach.

The nurses already knew the pros and cons of raising healthy children when caring for a cancer child. They had a few suggestions they had seen other families try. The healthy child or children could:

➢ Spend time at a relative's house
➢ Come along
➢ Bring a relative to you for tough treatment times

We could send Kate to a grandparent's or relative's house for the worst parts of the treatment. This would completely remove her from the world of cancer and her tired parents. She would most likely be the center of attention at their house and would probably be a lot of fun for the grandparents, aunts and uncles. Sending her to a relative's house for Bone Marrow Transplant (BMT), when we would be having a very tough month or two, would have been an ideal situation. Given a bit of preparation time for both Kate and the relatives, this could have been good for everyone. During BMT, we parents spent all our time either at the hospital or asleep. Siblings were not allowed in the BMT area and especially in the rooms of the patient. During this time of treatment and a few others, hanging out with family would have been the fairest to Kate. She would have stability and a schedule and be on vacation for most of it. Being so young, we did not have the additional worry of school.

The other option which applied to most of the normal treatment was to just drag Kate along with us to doctor appointments and hospital visits. Whenever possible we could have just taken her along. I saw several families do this during their journey. I kept thinking that this was nuts. How can you focus on the child with cancer AND the other children? This question is the whole point I was missing. I was not focusing on my other child at all. These other families were. **You can and should focus on both**. In fact, probably the healthiest thing to do for everyone involved is to broader the focus to the entire family whenever you can, not just the one sick member.

I am not saying that your healthy children are required to spend every moment in the hospital with your sick child. I am saying is that it is better to be inclusive when caring for all your children. Make a point to choose when your children join you at the hospitals. Choose the times they go to see relatives. Accept the fact that this world of cancer is your new normal. Make a plan that will include your healthy children and sick children that will show all of them that you care for them.

In our society, we make plans and perform research for most things in our children's lives. We pick schools; we choose what the kids do and where they play. We schedule play dates, other activities, and so on. I am suggesting we use that same method here in this situation. Decide to take your child with you to the hospital because it is good for the entire family to know what is happening there. Information is the best medicine for a bad attitude and a false impression of what is really happening at the hospital. Also, when it is better to leave the children with friends or relatives because they have had enough hospital time, then do so. Be inclusive and intentional, not exclusive and passive, with your children's care. There were times in Nathan's treatment that we included Kate in Nathan's care. It was in these times that things seemed to go the smoothest. Kate was happy and the most content. She was helpful and glad to see Nathan. Her bad moods were softer and easier to console. We also made time where Kate was the entire focus. She took dance classes and had recitals. She was in gymnastics and needed to go to class. In these instances, she was the center and we drug Nathan along when he was well enough to join us.

In our story, we chose the third option. During Nathan's worst treatment, Bone Marrow Transplant (BMT), we brought a grandparent to us. Scott's mother chose to use Family Medical Leave

Act (FMLA)[1] time to come to our house and help with Nathan and Kate's care. Grandma moved in with us at our house a month or so before Nathan was to be admitted for his BMT. That gave us time to acquaint Grandma with our schedule and Kate's care. It also gave Kate some time to get used to having Grandma around and figure out how she fit in the hierarchy of the family.

Figure 4 - Even with cancer in the house, there is time for dance recitals

---

[1] The following government websites gives specific guidelines for FMLA: https://www.dol.gov/general/topic/benefits-leave/fmla

This arrangement had several benefits to our family. Having one adult around all the time for Kate gave her some stability. Grandma could take Kate to daycare, which was now at our church and no longer on the Air Force base. She was also able to pick Kate up and make sure she was kept on some semblance of a schedule. With Grandma at the house, there was also a third set of hands to care for Nathan. During BMT there were a couple of times where Scott and I just bottomed out. We completely ran out of gas and needed a night of sleep at home. With preparation between us, the medical staff and Nathan, Grandma could cover a shift or two.

There were also several disadvantages to this relationship. When Nathan was evaluated for BMT he did not pass the criteria. He had too much disease left and the doctors feared that going into BMT with so much residual disease would leave him defenseless on the other side. If BMT did not get rid of all the bulky disease, then he could potentially have no immune system left to fight cancer. This would be a worst-case scenario without the possibility for survival. Grandma was already at our house when we found this out. So, while we assessed what to do with Nathan's care, Grandma stayed with us. This lead to a lot of confusion on Kate's side. Scott and I were around a lot, but so was Grandma. The roles and responsibilities became a bit muddled which was not helpful for Kate. To make this whole situation a little muddier, Scott and I did not do a good job clarifying our expectations well to Grandma or Kate.

However, once Nathan's BMT did arrive, Grandma was in place at the house and more than willing to help. Nathan had high dose metaiodobenzylguanidine (MIBG) therapy in Philadelphia, followed by BMT in Cincinnati. Scott, Nathan and I were gone for several weeks over these two treatments. Grandma was able to care for 2 years old Kate with us out of the way to remove the confusion. The two of them were able to bond a nice relationship during this time. The treatment took a couple of months and Grandma could spoil Kate and care for her without having to be a parent. She could stay Grandma. When Nathan finished his BMT, Grandma returned to her home and the four of us, Scott, Nathan, Kate and I, started to define our new normal life.

In this chapter, I have only listed three options that we saw in our lives. I am sure there are many other options out there or a combination of these. No matter what decision you make to care for your healthy kids while one is fighting cancer, there are several recommendations we have from our own experiences.

➤ Ask for and accept help. Family and friends will most likely ask you "What can I do to help you?" or "Let me know how I can help." Many of them actually expect you to answer them. They do not realize how difficult these questions can be. So, have some answers ready that are always true. Have some things that would be helpful but are not time constrained. For example, "If you have time, Kate would love to play someplace other than home." Or, "Kate would love a play date if you have some free time." Pick easy things for them to do and that will help you and you children. While Kate is at a play date, you can sleep. Or breath. Or have another cup of coffee.

➤ Openly communicate your expectations and needs to your helpers. If you choose to do things like us and bring in a grandparent for a couple of months, tell them up front what you will need from them. Explain to them that while you are at the hospital you will need them to take on a few parenting responsibilities with the healthy kids. Let them know whether you expect them to stay with you or at a hotel. It may be difficult to fully explain all your thoughts, but you have in your head what you want and need, so verbalize it. We did not do this well all the time, but when we did things worked very well. Early on my sister called and asked me when I needed her with us. I answered her honestly, "I need you here tomorrow." And I followed it up with specifics; "I need someone to love on Kate for a week. Her parents have vanished and she needs someone completely devoted to her until we can get back." My sister arrived a few days later. She knew what her role was, she was going to take care of Kate. She was staying a week. We would see her in the evenings when we all met back up at dinner and shared our days.

➤ Layout your specific plans. Include durations and expectations. "Mom, I need you here for a week." Or "Grandma, it will be great if you can stay with us for a month." The hardest part is defining an end to a visit or task after things have already started. If your children go to some grandparents set specific dates that you will pick them up. One problem we kept running into was not defining our expectations and needs to others well. We did not want to be bossy when folks were going to help us. We learned that the more specific you are, the easier it is for the helper to be successful and for you to return to caring for all your children. I have also learned how to be a better friend through this process. I no longer ask if I can help, I ask if I can bring a meal. Or I ask if the kids can come over to my house to play. Or I ask if they need some ice cream (everyone always needs ice cream). These are easy, helpful and uncomplicated things I can do for someone. Most importantly, all can be answered with a simple "yes" or "no".

➢ When you finally can care for your entire family again, do so. We had helpers come in and care for all of us, Scott, myself, the kids and themselves while visiting. It was an amazing blessing and I am forever humble that our families stepped up and sacrificed for us. Many of our visitors/helpers got into a similar routine. They would come visit us in the hospital. They would leave with plenty of time to get dinner figured out. Some would cook, some would buy dinner, but all of them had a meal ready for whichever parent went home that evening. Amazing blessings all of them! However, after over 18 months of fighting cancer 24 hours a day, 7 days a week, through front line therapy, 2 Bone Marrow Transplants, radiation and MIBG therapy, the day I remember the most was the day we declared ourselves out of panic mode. We decided that day we were finally to our new normal. From that point forward it was the four of us in the house with visitors to enjoy not only helpers we were in desperate need for.

Journaling

During our 10-year journey through the world of pediatric cancer treatment, we kept a journal. Four journals in its entirety. These books started as a way to exchange information between parents as we traded positions (home and hospital). As our story started before the age of Facebook, we also had a web based journal on CaringBridge.com to keep family and friends updated so we did not need to retell the same story or status several times a day.

As I prepared to write these two books, I reread the pages in our journals and relived each day they describe. The path through the journal leads through surgeries, chemotherapy, radiation treatment, bone marrow transplant twice and antibody therapy for Nathan. Then there is chicken pox, pneumonia, colds, the flu, broken bones, nose beads, chicken pox again, H1N1 flu a couple of times, accidents and other things for all of us.

Our first journal was a small empty book I found in the hospital gift shop. When that one was full, someone gave me another. Prior to MIBG and BMT therapy, we started a third so we had the information we needed for these complicated treatments at our finger tips. We had developed a layout we used to make finding information easier. We would tape business cards in the back pages. We listed labs we would need when we had them and any interesting results. Nathan drew on several pages as did Kate. I recorded scans in them so I could show Scott what I saw. It was a little life line where I could dump all my raw emotions. Something about writing your feelings down on paper to capture them. It allows you to let go for a little while and move forward with caring for your family. Friends and families would write messages in the journals for us. Words of encouragement and prayers that we could read whenever we had a free moment.

The one thing that comes out the most to me as I see our past 10 years is how much our daughter Kate helped us in it all. You can read the more she was included the more we all got along. You can read how much we missed her when she was not around. In these journals, the amount we love this little girl is obvious. When she is older I will let her read them herself.

We recommend a journal for any family fighting any long-term battle. The stories are raw but honest. They capture the events, emotions and activities much more accurately than my memory. They allowed a place for people to leave prayers that we could read whenever we needed support. The journals gave us a place to capture all the caregiving information, such that we could then sleep. They were a much-needed constant in a life filled with uncertainty and chaos.

Routine

A family may no longer have access to their old way of life, but that does not stop them from creating a new way of life. Our family was having a tough time adjusting to our new reality. Everything was new and out of place in our lives. To get some sort of control and sanity back we tried to find some form of routine to follow. Our schedule needed to include Nathan's trips to the hospital for treatment and those additional visits to the hospital for a fever. We also had to include Scott's work and Kate's care. Me staying home with her full time was no longer an option for our family, so we needed to find stability for her day to day. Additionally, we thought it would be very nice if we could find a way for both parents to get some sleep somewhere, sometime.

We hated the feeling of chaos and lack of control in everything. We understood cancer was going to be difficult, but that did not mean we had to let go and allow it to completely overshadow the simplest of tasks. We were strongly motivated to get out of "panic" mode and into a sustainable lifestyle. That included eating, sleeping and exercise. Panic mode inherently puts all daily activates on the back burner. In panic mode, it does not matter what you eat, just that you do eat. It does not matter how much or where you sleep, just that you do. In panic mode, exercise and personal care do not happen. If cancer was going to take years, we needed to get out of panic mode and into a sustainable and flexible routine.

After several attempts, Scott and I finally found a routine that worked for us for most of Nathan's standard treatments. We were a couple of months into treatment, Kate had started to attend a childcare center and Scott was back at work. Those days that Nathan was at the hospital, after a full day of work, Scott would come to the hospital in the evening with Kate. We would have a moment or two to chat and then I would take Kate home so Scott could take care of Nathan through the night. The next morning Kate and I would arrive back at the hospital to swap back again. Scott would take Kate to daycare then go to work while I would stay with Nathan that day and through the night. The next night we would repeat this cycle. This routine could go on for weeks depending on how long Nathan was in treatment or recovering from a fever. This routine helped define our responsibilities and gave us some stability for this stage of life while allowing us to get rid of the chaos feeling. Anything in the battle with cancer that fell outside of our routine would be handled on its own. This routine got us through front line therapy and several other treatments.

Having a routine does not accommodate all aspects of life. Even with a routine, each child will need direct quality time with parents and siblings. Just going through the steps does not fulfill the parenting each child needs. I mentioned earlier my evening walks with Kate in the stroller. Kate would get angry with even the smallest of interruptions. I admit I probably did not handle it in the best way for long term development of our relationship. I was with her on the walk, but I was not parenting her. She had my body, but not my presence. I have since come up with an alternate scenario that will illustrate what I mean. When walking and friends came to chat with us, I could have picked Kate up out of the stroller and let the neighbor dote on her. This would inherently change the conversation from Nathan and cancer to Kate and cuteness. It would put her in the center of attention instead of just "shushing" her when she got fussy. It would have calmed me down, calmed her down and entertained the neighbor. It would probably have also taught her a method for resolving her issues with kindness and fun instead of tantrums and anger. When we got home, I should have put myself in her play space and taken my place as mom and best playmate a child could have. I should have chatted with her, or given her all my attention even if just for a small time. I was home with her to spend time with her and instead of making that a priority I took the easy path of little crying and little conflict. Would she have been mad at me if I had spun her around several times and just made her laugh? She now says she would not have.

We did learn that being inclusive when handling our children made things simpler. When with Kate, I focus on her. I needed to get rid of my preconceived before cancer ideas of parenting and come up with a new plan for my family. In our society, there is a lot of information about how to raise children. A lot of pressure to treat children a certain way to make them stronger, better adjusted and whatever else the masses decide. It is easy to fall into the trap of trying to parent your child according to societies expectations. It is easy to feel the pressure of what is the "best" way to raise children. However, this set of rules and lessons does not work in a normal life, let alone in the world of cancer. I needed to make a plan for our family and situation. A routine was the first step to succeeding in this.

Open Communication

Throughout this book, I will discuss keeping your healthy children involved in the care of your sick child. Independent of the age of the children, either older or younger than the child with cancer, they can be a wonderful resource in caring for a sick child. Siblings will naturally ignore as much of the serious stuff going on as they can. They will ignore the tubes and machines attached to their sibling while running down the hallway. Nathan liked to assign the care of his medicine/pump pole, called R2D2, to his grandfather so that he and his sister could run down the hospital hallway chasing Silly Putty. The doctor, nurses and I cringed at all the germs getting on that ball of Silly Putty, but the smiles and laughter far out weighted the germs. Some hand washing to remove the germs from the kids and throwing away that silly putty when done to remove the germs on it and they were good as new.

Part of keeping children involved is having some forum for open communication. Over our 10-year duration of actively treating Neuroblastoma, Kate grew from a 1-year-old baby to an 11-year-old young lady. We did not discuss with the 1-year-old baby the same things we can now discuss with the much older sister. Our daughter absorbs various aspects of Nathan's illness as she grows older. As a baby, we talked about Nathan being sick and in the hospital. We talked about not pulling on any of his tubes and lines. We talked about letting him sleep when he was not feeling great. We discussed things that would make sense to a little girl. As she got older we could explain in greater detail how sick Nathan had really been.

It would have been unfair and probably terrifying to tell a very young Kate that we were afraid her brother was not going to live to go to Kindergarten. Telling her something so awful would have served no good purpose for anyone. However, as she has gotten older, in her angrier moments she makes fun of Nathan having some remaining issues with cancer side effects, like weak legs and hearing aids. This is when we can let her know why Nathan has these issues and they really are not something to tease him about. Kate was 10 years old before we told her that Nathan almost died. To my surprise, she went to her room and cried for over an hour. Teasing your brother is one thing that all sisters will do, but realizing you almost did not have this brother around to pester really hit a soft spot in Kate.

Every parent must decide to what level a child needs to know the details of their sibling's disease. I suggest caution with the harsher details. Find ways to say things to little kids that make your point, but does not scare them. Try to avoid saying things like "be careful around Nathan, if he gets sick he will need to go to the hospital." Or "germs can kill him." Instead, say things like "Let us go wash our hands. They are pretty dirty." Avoid an extreme message that your healthy children will take very literally and hold onto. You can easily scare your kids with a harsh comment that will impact them for a long time. At this point, it would be better to team up with your children instead of fighting them. Have conversations where you can be a team: "Let us get this house cleaned so Nathan can stay home from the hospital longer this time." An "us VS cancer" attitude is much healthier for all. The finger pointing comments to not get your sibling sick is an attitude that helps no on. It is better for all that children to know what is going on with their sick sibling, but in words, they can understand and process. Give them things they can help with but will not scare them. The entire cancer thing is scary enough. The word itself can incite images of their sibling dying. We avoided the cancer word around Kate until she was much older. We called Nathan's disease Neuroblastoma, which to a young child does not equate to cancer.

Please, remember, your healthy children only know as much as you tell them about the sibling's disease. They need to have enough information to be able to help care for them even if it is just sitting in bed with them watching TV. They do not need so much information that they are afraid to be around them.

Programs for Kids

Many times, when a family loses a child to cancer, they create organizations to help all families going through the same fight. Several organizations found us and offered a little respite:

- Children's Neuroblastoma Cancer Foundation (CNCF) - teaches parents about the disease and treatment options as well as raise funds to support promising treatment options.
- Hospital Social workers and Child Life Experts – spend their entire careers making children's time in the hospital as smooth with as little stress as possible so the families can concentrate on care for the child.
- Ronald McDonald House – An amazing organization that provides rooms, food and facilities (at a reasonable price) for families that are receiving care away from their home.
- Candlelighters – in many hospitals provide educational materials for newly diagnosed families and support for parents.
- Corporate Angel Network – companies that allow sick children and a care giver to fly on their corporate airplanes for transport to treatments.
- Project Angel Hugs - sends gifts to children with cancer and their siblings.

> ➢ Special Wish Foundation and Make a Wish Foundation – provide once in a lifetime trips and gifts to children who have a life-threatening disease.
> ➢ Give Kids the World – a resort in Florida that pairs up with Wish foundations to provide an amazing family experience in Orlando Florida.
> ➢ Waves of Hope in Florida - take children with cancer and siblings boating for the day. Local boat owners plan a boat outing. They pick up kids and their siblings and parents at the marina. They show them a day of boating, BBQ and beach fun. Kate got to go as her own person, she was not just Nathan's sister.
> ➢ Our local Optimist Club – Held parties for children with cancer and siblings where they can create their own unique Build-a-Bear.

In addition to all these resources, there are even some hospitals have a summer camp for Hematology/Oncology patients. In Cincinnati, it was called Camp Joy (Camp EnjoyItAll) The camp has doctors and nurses there on site 24 hours a day, 7 days a week, to administer medications and care for any ailment. No parents attend. The kids get to be kids for a whole week with other kids that are just like them. Their siblings were also allowed to attend this camp. Sibling lives have not been easy either. If the camps allow siblings, let them go. They will have time to see their sick brother or sister looking well and doing normal things. That will be good for all of them.

Find organizations that see siblings as cherished friends. The folks who volunteer their time and resources to these ventures have told us that nothing makes the people of these organizations happier than to utilize their gifts and offerings. There are several programs for kids related to someone fighting cancer or long-term illnesses. Please take advantage of the resources available to them.

These are just a few we have been privileged to work with. Organizations are out there that LOVE to spoil kids. Check with your hospital staff to see what is available in your area and how they can participate. Check with your child's doctor to make sure they are well enough to participate, but, in general, any distraction during treatment is a good thing.

More detailed information about these organizations and others can be found in CHAPTER 10.

NOTES

NOTES

CHAPTER 4. "I WANT HER TO HAVE A NORMAL LIFE"

My family's entire world changed the day Nathan was diagnosed with cancer. Our well-planned life was thrown into chaos. Our days were no longer spent together Mom, Dad, Nathan and Kate, but were transformed into a quick education about medicine, the human body and time management. Gone were the times spent wandering the neighborhood playing with friends, digging in the dirt and growing up. These times were replaced with a sense of panic that germs were everywhere. No longer are leaves to be jumped in, but avoided. Now those same leaves contain fungus, which could kill our son. We knew Nathan's life was forever changed but did Kate's life also need to change?

Our first gut reaction, when given this diagnosis of cancer, was to make Kate's life "as normal" as possible. Nathan, Mom and Dad were going to be sucked into this battle, maybe we could keep Kate out of it. Maybe she could still have the normal life we had planned for her. She is just one-year old. We could protect her. We could cherish her. She did not need to know about needles, nasty medicines, surgery and all the fear. One of the four of us could make it through this battle unscarred. One of us could be untouched by the awful disease of cancer. And that one should be Kate. What could possibly be wrong with this idea? I must admit, after a 10-year battle with cancer, this plan for Kate could never work and was unfair to her to try.

We were so naive in our thinking of what fighting cancer would mean to our family. There is no way to have Kate live in our world and not be affected by cancer. The caregiver and the sick person can be at the hospital several days in a row. Other times it is just many hours in the day. There is no way to hold onto a "normal" life (aka life before cancer) when you have such a severe disruption. I must admit we really tried. We brought in family members to take care of Kate, we had friends take care of Kate, we made her schedules try to resemble our pre-cancer schedules as much as possible. We juggled people, we manipulated situations. We did everything we could think of to keep her life normal. However, in the end we learned that life could not be "normal" for Kate. We had missed the one thing she wanted most of all from her family, and that was to be with her family. She had spent the first year of her life with us and now we, her family, had vanished. The things that we did to normalize her life just accentuated the fact that her life was not going to be the same.

Figure 5 - Kate finding normal life in hot pink jacket and blue shoes as Nathan gets on the bus for kindergarten

In hindsight, it would have been better for everybody if we just embraced this earlier and accepted the fact that our lives had changed and that nothing was going to be the same or "normal". Everything was now different in the darker light of a serious illness. If we had accepted this earlier and adapted to it, our handling of Kate would have been better. In our attempts to make her life normal we alienated her and set her aside from the rest of her family. There is no surprise that she grew angry with her family.

As I described earlier, Kate acted out in severe ways to get our attention (yelling, kicking, tantrums, biting, screaming, etc.). It became a horrible spiral. We went to such extremes to make her life normal. This in turn made ourselves even more tired and exhausted and therefore even more unavailable to her. Which made her act out even more. Kate learned to get our attention by misbehaving. When she acted in a normal way for a one-year-old, we just kind of smoothed over them. She is a very smart young lady and realized that when she used extreme behavior the only way we could pacify her would be to focus completely on her. She learned what worked were screaming fits for over an hour, or not taking naps for over a week which would then put her in the even worse mood and worst behavior. An all-out war of disobedience and defiant behavior was the best way she could get her parents full and undivided attention.

Kate was most likely predisposed to a defiant attitude, but she is also a deeply caring child. She is exceptional at looking after younger children and finding ways to include them in activities. A few years into Nathan's treatment we realize how Kate cared for people and included her more. This did not change her behavior immediately. In fact, it took years of effort to get her to a place where she would start trying to communicate with her family using methods that are not screaming, yelling, crying, throwing tantrums and fits. I feel at our current stage in our lives together we have open communication we can now talk through problems. However, her immediate reaction to anything negative from a parent, a loved one or friend is immediately a defensive attitude. She will start arguing; she will assume the worst possible intentions initially and generally will get angry and either stomp off or act out. When she was younger, this could go on for hours. Now, as she is getting older, she takes a moment or two, then returns, gives a hug and talks it out, some of the times.

Since part of her natural personality is to be more defensive and assume negative things when people are speaking to her, by excluding her in in Nathan's care we escalated this behavior. Our actions would feed her negative assumptions about things. If we were late to get her, she would assume we were having fun without her. Not that Nathan's care took extra time or that we fell asleep. When things did not go as she had expected, she would immediately lash out about how unfair this was and how we did not love her. Mind you in most instances where this happed we did not actually know what she expected to happen. Sometimes it was as simple as we did not walk in the correct direction, or we did not cook her what she wanted to eat. Now that she is nearing her teenage years we feel we have given her some tools to help overcome these tendencies. She can now see when her attitude is getting in the way of her seeing things clearly, and chooses to take some time to cool her anger down before lashing out. She has learned how to talk with her parents without the fear of getting yelled at or reprimanded. She now recovers from an anger episode faster and comes out calmer and ready to talk things through. Now, after she and I have a disagreement, she will come over to me and give me a hug, and apology with a desire to discuss whatever it was that caused the argument. She still likes to us the phrase "That's not fair", but now many times after a moment or two to calm down, we can talk through what unfair means. But there are still times she just cannot recover and cannot control her anger or actions.

Now that we know what our lives look like 10 years down our path, the one question that comes to mind often is: "How would we have done it differently?" If we could go back and redo things with all the knowledge that we have gained from going through this once, what would we have changed? Would it have made a difference? Would it be worth the effort?

I would have included Kate more and allow her natural tendencies to let us escape cancer for a few moments when with her. I would be more deliberate in Kate's care where I allowed her to join us at the hospital a frequently as I could but still gave her respite from cancer by having her visit friends and family. I honestly believe this different approach would have given her perspective on the difficulties of having a sick family member. No matter the outcome, it would certainly have been worth the effort to try a more team orientated family approach to battling cancer.

Through Nathan's cancer, we were given an opportunity to teach Kate about empathy for other people. Allowing her to participate in Nathan's care would allow her to be part of the family. She would see how people lovingly care for each other. Kate could have learned by watching her brother be sick and how he handled it. With a loving hand by her family to give her involvement, information and knowledge Kate could have been shown how to have empathy for not only her brother but everybody else. We feel the best thing that we could have done for Kate with her strong personality and tendency towards the negative was to give her a chance to care for her brother and love on him. We could have shown her how to put someone else first. We could have shown her what a loving family does when faced with adversity and crisis. We could have shown her how to face her battles head on. She could have learned at an early age how to truly care about others and be a loving caring compassionate individual. An attitude of "Let us together care for your brother" would have served her well.

There is no one normal life. You are given one life by God. Due to circumstances, we cannot understand, this world has horrible things happen to young children. It is our responsibility to find a way to handle these situations to the best of your ability while showing God's love to the people around us. Including all the people and children we meet along our path. Our children get one childhood. It is our job as their parents to guide them through it. We are to show them how to be God loving adults. This cannot be done if their lives are put on hold while caring for another child.

I have been reading our journals to prepare for this book. I realize how tired and exhausted, overwhelmed and hurt we all were. We were in a complete state of disarray and had no idea what to do next for Nathan not to mention what we should have done next for Kate. It was also obvious that we did not ignore or bypass Kate. We incorrectly chose to exclude her for the reasons I have mentioned. As I have said, we thought we were sacrificing to give her a better life. We feel if we had been more intentional with Kate's inclusion in Nathan's care from the beginning, Kate would be a more comfortable person in her surroundings and world, now.

In our journals, one thing keeps coming out over and repeatedly. We constantly talk about how Kate is our bright shiny spot. We talk about how Kate makes everybody happy. We talk about how Kate keeps us sane. We talk about her being our escape from cancer. We talk about how Kate makes the time go by faster. We talk about how much better Nathan feels when Kate is around. We talk about how Nathan recovers from treatments quicker with Kate so he can go play with her. We talk about how Kate distracts us from what ails us and distracts us from the world of cancer.

That is why we know that including Kate would have been better for all four of us. Granted, spending more time with Kate would have taken some of the attention away from Nathan, but taking an hour here and there away from staring at our sick son and playing with our vibrant young daughter could not hurt anyone. In fact, it probably would have revitalized us daily. The little energy it would have taken to include Kate, to hold her and make her stop being mad at me, would probably have made the rest of the day easier, not harder.

Kate and I eventually got to a point where our interactions were full of conflicts. One of Kate's and my constant conflicts was over sleep. I remember day in and day out just trying to find a way to sleep. I was always looking for a place that I could take a one-hour nap, or a 30-minute nap, or a 15-minute power nap, something. Always trying to find time and place where Kate could go so that I could nap. As I mentioned earlier, she refused to nap anytime or anywhere. She would constantly cry whenever I put her in her crib or bed. It was impossible to sleep over her very strong lungs. In my exhausted state, the internal guilt would flow. "I should be in there calming her." "I should do something to help her sleep." My exhausted brain could not come up with an answer.

In our society with the constant bombardment of parenting advice, a new mom hears all the time that children need to find a way to comfort themselves. They need to learn how to sleep in their own beds. They need to learn how to put themselves to sleep without being rocked by mom or dad each night. This way of thinking does not apply to a cancer family. The answer to my sleep dilemma is so obvious now, even though I could not see it then. The answer is we should have napped together. Kate and I should have run our errands together. She should have been dragged to the hospital and taught how to deal with being bored at the hospital together.

Figure 6 - Kate enjoying the zoo

I remember at the time thinking that I did not have one more ounce of energy to give to anybody. I was so tired and so exhausted and I had nothing left. I needed someone to regenerate me. As I have matured in my faith and matured as a person I realize that the best way to regenerate oneself and to fix oneself is to give more to others. Who better to give it to but a one-year-old little girl who just wants to hang out with her family, maybe visit the zoo or park sometime. For our daughter, Kate does not want to just hang out with her family she wants to control her family and have them do whatever she wants them to do. And that is exactly what a one-year-old little girl is supposed to do. It is in spending time with her that we teach her to do things differently and smooth the edges of her personality.

Figure 7 - Kate learning that time-outs also come on vacations

In general, children need to learn boundaries and natural consequences. They must know there is a consequence for their actions. For example, when a child is misbehaving as the family is preparing for a fun activity like going to the beach on vacation taking a time out from activities to give them a chance to settle and think about things, is a natural consequence of their actions. Even this needs to be balanced for a family fighting cancer. Yes, time to think and dwell and a bit of understanding from their parents can be beneficial to an agitated child. But, they still need to have a set of rules. This applies to the sick child as well.

Somewhere during Nathan's treatment, we realized that when cancer was no longer part of our lives (one way or the other) we were going to have a daughter who had a completely different experience than the rest of her family. She would not remember the long nights at the hospital because she was not there. She would not remember her parents crying themselves to sleep because we did not let her see it. She would not remember how close we were to losing her brother because she was not involved in his care and did not know how serious it was. This was not going to be a good thing for our family.

We as a family (Kate included) have decided that we are in all our battles together. Now we drag Kate along whenever we can and when she is not needed at school, orchestra or sports. We make a point of showing her that her activities are just as important as Nathan's doctor appointments and Nathan's activities. We all go to Kate's hockey games, even Nathan, sometimes. There are softball games to cheer at, orchestra concerts to listen to, ice skating on a sunny summer Saturday afternoon and so on. We all listen to Kate learn every musical instrument she can (Double bass, cello, violin, ukulele, flute, recorder, electric bass guitar and piano, to name a few). Kate is no longer shushed, she is embraced, enjoyed and supported. Now, this is our actual normal.

Even today, Nathan continues to have many late effects show up without warning. A few weeks ago, he had a spontaneous collapsed lung. We found ourselves immediately going back to our old ways of finding a place for Kate then taking Nathan to the hospital. This time we noticed and stopped. This time she came along with us. She made the most wonderful comment that made us realize that we had turned a corner when caring for Kate. The night Nathan's lung collapsed Kate looked at me very seriously and said: "you know Mom, most families when they plan to go canoeing with the Boy

Scouts, actually go canoeing with the Boy Scouts." ..... but not ours was the part she had left out. She was not mad, or angry, just making an observation that our family's normal was very different than other families' normal, but that is just the life she has been given. She seems to be accepting that her family's normal is fine with her.

NOTES

CHAPTER 5. "I DO NOT WANT TO EXPOSE HER TO THE HOSPITAL"

Before our son Nathan was diagnosed with cancer, I felt the hospital was a terrifying place. There are scary germs everywhere. There are scary tests, scans and mysterious treatments. Doctors and nurses all seemed foreign and difficult to talk with. Little kids could get in the way, get hurt or get sick. When we visited a hospital, my objective was always to get out of the hospital as fast as possible. So, when Nathan was diagnosed, it is exactly where I did not want my daughter to be. A hospital is a place where you go in, you have done whatever it is you need to have done and you go home. No place for a baby unless she is sick, really sick.

Over the past 10 years, I learned our assumptions about hospitals are not always true. Granted a hospital is still a place you need to take seriously. It is still filled with scary germs. There still are scary tests and scans. However, the doctors and nurses are not nearly as terrifying as expected. I can now speak with them in a way we both, sort of, understand. The doctors and nurses in the world of Oncology are sweet and loving. They care for their patients, the parents and the other children. When a patient's sibling comes to the hospital, the patient is in much better spirits. The patient brags about their sibling and tells the hospital staff all the wonderful things they can do. Yes, the little ones can escape from time to time, but generally, they are scooped back up and brought back to the room in the arms of a nurse or aide.

Having his sibling around helped Nathan heal a lot more than it hurt us. When Kate came to the hospital she demanded attention. She demanded it from her parents, from Nathan and from the staff. She refused to just sit in the room and watch TV. She forced Nathan and her parents out of the room. We had to go to the play room. We had to go see every fish tank in the hospital. We had to go outside to swing on the swings. All with her sick brother in tow. As Nathan puts it, when Kate came to the hospital we had to see everything it had to offer. No more sitting in the room feeling sorry for ourselves.

When Kate did visit the hospital, no one could feel sorry for themselves or each other. No one could just sit around and dwell on our situation. Everyone had to pay attention to Kate. What an amazing blessing that was. She demanded we get outside of ourselves. She forced us to realize the world would continue while we were in the hospital. We could either make the best of it or not. Kate forced us to make the best it. Granted, this meant more work for mom and dad. This meant we had to depend on others sometimes. We would occasionally need to leave Nathan alone to sleep in his room while we escorted Kate to the gift shop, the cafeteria or walk around the hospital to find the baby fish in all the fish tanks. Yes, Kate got sick on occasion, but the benefits were so obvious and so beneficial to everyone.

Kate learned a lot from the experience. Before spending time in the hospital, she had it in her mind that the hospital was fun and exciting. She thought all we did there was play and visit and have a wonderful time. After spending time in the hospital with us, she learned that the hospital was boring. It stunk, quite literally it smelled. Most of the things they do to you in the hospital hurt. They give you shots. They boss you around. They are working and do not have time for siblings all the time. Kate learned empathy and kindness when she visited. She learned to manage her situation and always have something with her to help avoid the boredom of the hospital. She also learned that sometimes she did just want to stay home or go to a friend's house.

There were several times in Nathan's journey that Kate proved to be the best cure for anything that ailed him. One stands out most prominently during Bone Marrow Transplant. Bone Marrow Transplant (BMT), also called stem cell rescue, was the longest and most difficult part of Nathan's treatment. In general, the child is in the hospital for at least 30 days. They need to stay near the BMT hospital for an additional 30 to 60 days, depending on how they recover. This is one area of treatment and recovery that we had little choice for Kate's care. She was not allowed on the BMT floor at the hospital and she was not allowed to see Nathan. They could visit via computer and video conferencing, but only when Nathan felt up for it. During BMT Nathan was awful to watch. We needed to find a way to help him. Having Kate around always made Nathan feel better and made Kate smile. We needed to get the two of them together physically.

After the worst part of BMT when Nathan was recovering from his pain, he hit a plateau or road block to his recovery. Nothing made him smile. He did not eat; he did not drink; he never left his bed; he was lethargic and pathetic. He had even stopped talking to Kate on the computer. To illustrate how bad Nathan was feeling, here is a journal entry from that time:

Journal Entry: *"Up until now, whenever I arrive at the hospital Nathan would usually hunt through my back pack to see what cool toys and things I had brought for him. He would stop all conversation until the back pack was COMPLETELY emptied and checked a few times, then he would continue on his way (he loves getting stuff no matter how small; he is four; go figure). Now for the perspective: Nathan has three boxes, one package and one card that sits unopened beside his BMT bed. He just does not feel well enough to care about them yet. Oh, he will and we will tear through them, but we are just not there yet."*

We talked with Nathan's primary BMT doctor about Kate coming to visit. She needed special permission because children younger than 7 years old were not allowed on the BMT floor at this hospital. Kate was just 2 years old at the time. Nathan's primary BMT doctor decided it would be safe and we received special permission for her visit.

When Kate arrived in Nathan's room, Nathan was just lying in bed staring blankly at the TV. Kate came over, climbed into bed with him and took his blanket. She then requested or demanded that he watch Little Einsteins (HER favorite show). Nathan turned the channel for her. Kate started to jabber at him. Nathan started to smirk. Then he started to smile. As the show played for a little bit, the Little Einsteins said: *"Pat, pat, pat, Blast off."* By this point, Nathan had a big smile on his face, had his arms in the air with Kate and was yelling at the top of his lungs *"BLAST OFF."* At that moment, our happy little boy returned for good. As soon as the show ended Kate looked at the stack of unwrapped packages. "What's in those?" she asked. The two of them then tore through the gifts laughing and smiling as they went. We knew then, thanks to his sister, Kate, Nathan was going to be just fine.

Figure 8 - Pat, Pat, Pat, BLAST OFF!

I realize that there are several times in a child's treatment for cancer that there is not a place for a little girl running around. However, there are many more times where a little girl running around would be the best medicine for child and parent alike.

During BMT we met a family who had a daughter going through a BMT also. She was about his age and was admitted to the hospital the same day as Nathan. This family did things completely differently than we did. This family had several children and the youngest was born while their sister was completing her BMT. This family not only professed their faith in Jesus and wore their Christianity on their sleeves, but they also completely included their children in the care of their daughter and sister. One or more of the children were at every chemotherapy treatment. When the baby arrived, the whole family would be involved in caring for the baby and the sister. When I talked with the children they were very matter-of-fact about the whole situation and were completely well adjusted. I have followed this family since and not only did the daughter survive her cancer treatment, but the family is thriving. They are now a strong advocate nationally for Bone Marrow Donors.

This is the family I wanted to be like. I had a firm faith in Jesus but did not profess it everywhere I went. I loved my children but did not include our daughter in our son's care. Granted, this mother looked as tired and exhausted as I did. She looked at the end of her physical rope but her spiritual strength carried her entire family. She was a delight to spend time with and talk to. Now I see this woman and family as a message from God of the way I could have it all. With God's help and this family's example, I saw how I could care for my entire family and we could all thrive

NOTES

NOTES

CHAPTER 6. "I JUST DON'T HAVE THE ENERGY"

It is true that when caring for a sick loved one, whether a child or parent, you, the caregiver, may find yourself eternally exhausted. Thinking about how to take in a quick nap is the one thing on the forefront of your mind at all times. You start dreaming about how comfortable a chair would be and if I just lay my head against the wall it will be the best feeling ever. Just closing your eyes and letting a dream state come over you would be just the best thing. As one of Nathan's caregivers, this thought would consume me. Watching my child lay in bed being very sick took every last drop of energy out of me. I could not imagine how adding a baby or child to this state of exhaustion could even happen. However, I propose here that it is exactly the thing you and your healthy children need most.

As I mentioned earlier, children have a way of demanding your attention. That is their job. It is your job to raise them and love them. They need and deserve any attention you may have for them. Sitting watching your child be sick will take a lot more energy from you than playing with your healthy child. Exhaustion can consume you. Where and when is it the right time to nap? When is the right time to play? When is the right time to pray while watching your sick child? There needs to be a balance with all of these.

I know that there were times I did not actually have the ability to get up and play without napping first. I remember laying down on the floor in the play room at the hospital where I had Kate surrounded in a corner. I passed out. She played. If she tried to get past me I would wake up. There were several times where she spent the entire play time talking (jabbering) at me. I smiled and passed out. She would talk and poke me. I would wake up, smile and pass out. We spent a couple of hours like this. She has told me that this type of playing was so much better than being at the day care where she had all the toys in the world. Being here with her mother even though her mother could not keep her eyes open was better. I was very careful that every time she woke me I did not grumble at her. I would answer her question in my sleepy voice, kiss her hand and pass back out. We were in a safe place. I knew if she got past me a staff member would scoop her up and return her to me.

There were other times where Kate needed to go to the playground and run. Nathan was placed in a wagon and went along. Kate spent time in a swing. Nathan was next to her in the special swing for kids who cannot hold on by themselves. Scott pushed them both and we all just breathed. I do not want to imply any of this is easy, but I do propose for the sake of everyone involved, to include your healthy child (or children) whenever you can. Take some specific time to spend with them either at the hospital or at home. Show your healthy children how much they matter to you. Having a team mentality can help. Instead of finding a place for your children to go so you can run errands take them with you. Errand running can be just as fun as a play date if it is with your parents you have not seen in a while.

It is easy to get caught up in the intensity of caring for a sick child and pass over the easier healthy children. Try to explain to your kids in words that they can understand (age appropriate) what is going on and why you are away so much. Explain how they can help you and their sibling and then give them the opportunity to try. Tell them that the time you two are together (even if in a hospital) you both can help each other. Include them in the care. The two of you can take care of your sick child together. You children can help your sick child by watching TV with them or playing a simple board game or even them playing a video game may give your brain and heart a break. Mario Kart was a hospital favorite since four of us could play at the same time together. You never know, you may just get the opportunity to rest your head against the wall and sleep. Your children may also get the opportunity to create a relationship that can carry them through their lifetimes. Adding your healthy children into the care of your sick child it will take effort, but you will be surprised when the healthy child grows up how they remember those moments together as a family as the best times no matter where they took place.

Even though Kate was very young during the worst part of Nathan's treatment she remembers the time we spent together. She does not remember any of her time at the day care. She remembers only a few times with family and friends. But she can tell me EVERY time I took her to the hospital or on a walk or to the mall. She can tell me all the times that we shared in the care of Nathan. She can describe all the hospital play rooms where she helped me nap. She can describe the fish tanks and the kind of fish they contained. She even remembers the number of baby fish in each. I must assume this means that those times are the most important and most precious to her.

Nathan tells me constantly the stories of Kate at the hospital with him. He does not remember chemotherapy at any of the four hospitals he received therapy, but he remembers wandering the hospitals with Kate looking for fish. The hospital of his diagnosis had fish tanks in several locations. No matter how sick he was, he and Kate would go visit the fish to make sure they were all ok.

Nathan does not remember Bone Marrow Transplant, but he remembers shooting his Long Shot Nerf gun with Dad and Kate at hospital staff. Right after Bone Marrow Transplant when Kate visited, Nathan was allowed an outing from his hospital room. Nathan, Kate and Scott took Nathan's Long Shot Nerf gun into the hallway. They took up a spot on a blanket on the floor. With help, Nathan and Kate took turns shooting the gun down the hallway to see who could shoot it the furthest. Staff members would accidentally walk into the nerf darts as they left the rooms of other children. This brought on great laughter from Nathan, Kate and Scott (by the way, laughter is great for the lungs).

Nathan does not remember antibody therapy in New York City, but he does remember the times he could show Kate the American Museum of Natural History. Nathan had several treatments in New York City. When he was not recovering from a treatment we would walk around the area we were staying in the city. He was always looking for places to show Kate for the times she joined us there. The American Museum of Natural History was his favorite. Nathan loved dinosaurs and he needed to show them to Kate as often as he could.

Nathan remembers Kate crawling into bed with him and watching TV. Nathan remembers Kate taking over the play room at the hospital. He also remembers those baby fish they would count. He remembers the visits to a gift shop to waste time which included a list of things that Kate would like if we were to buy them for her. The list goes on and on.

These examples confirm, we could have made both of their lives better and ours less exhausting by including Kate more in Nathan's care. If we were more inclusive with raising both of our children and not succumbing to the chaos that surrounds any horrible disease we could redefine our normal life to include both kids no matter how much energy it required.

NOTES

CHAPTER 7. "LATER I WILL FIX IT"

"I need to focus on our son now, later I will fix any harm or problems we caused our daughter." I found myself saying something like this whenever things got "tough" during treatment. It was easier to push off what I could not handle without evaluating the consequences. Daily activities would occur where decisions had to be made about Nathan's care, battling cancer, and Kate's care, not battling cancer. In this perspective, your focus must be on the child fighting cancer. While that is true when decisions must be made about treatment and cater, it is less true when things are proceeding according to a plan. I completely agree, there were times where nothing entered my brain except thinking about Nathan treatment options. But frequently this intense time turns into the daily minutia of medicine schedule and other more mundane aspects of his care. In these times please focus on the needs of the healthy children.

Now, I must say from experience that it is not possible to fix ANY and ALL problems your healthy children may experience. You cannot untrain a child that they were not important during the care of your sick child. You cannot get enough therapy for the family to completely undo the hurt you cause them during this time. Those underlying feelings of being inadequate, being unimportant, needing to act out to get your parent's attention do not go away. You cannot erase these things. This is the childhood you may be giving them; you need to make sure you raise them to be confident adults. Eventually, cancer will be out of your life. You do not want to lose your other child or children in the process.

I realize these are very harsh statements. Nothing can be that dire and that definitive. Everything can be fixed or at least that is the philosophy of our culture. However, I disagree.

Your children grow up with the experiences you give them. Children will know if they were important to you or not even though you are caring for a sick child. Children are very observant and even if the child says hurtful things about spending too much time at the hospital, about being bored, about the unfairness of it, they will know if you gave them the best childhood you could in the situation you were given. If your children do not experience the same life that you are experiencing while caring for a sick child it is because you are not letting them. Your children will only have the experiences you let them have. With no other input, they will base their opinions on what they see, how they feel, or they will just fill the details in as they want. The one thing that will be clear to them is that you were missing. I have asked Kate what she remembers about Nathan being sick. The one thing she remembers the most is that her family was missing and never around her.

As I have mentioned before, Kate saw Nathan's time at the hospital differently than we did. When we left her with friends and family we felt we were keeping her from all this awful stuff. However, in her mind, with nothing to compare it to, she thought Nathan and I were having a party every day we were there. Otherwise, why would we keep her away when she made us all so happy?

People learn from the experience they have and see. They can learn great understanding, caring, empathy, tolerance and the ability to adapt to weird surroundings. This can be part of their makeup of their being. This happens when children are shown things from their parents and family. In our family, Nathan learned these things from his sister. She was the spark, the escape from his reality. However, Kate did not learn these things during Nathan's time in the hospital because we did not show them to her.

The point of this book is to help parents to try to avoid these issues. I wish I knew how this would affect Kate and how I could have made it better. I wish someone had told me the things I have included in this book. But no one did or if they did I did not listen.

Kate, Scott, Nathan and I have started the process to repair the years of exclusion for Kate. We talk about everything we can get her to talk about. We declare a free talk time where she can say anything, no matter how awful it may sound, without any chance of punishment or discipline. Every day I tell her how happy I am that she is in my life. Even when she is acting out, when we have raised voices, I let her know that "even this is better than you not being in my life." We are making it work as a family. She is responding and adapting to how our life is normal. It has taken many years and a LOT of hard work to get Kate here. I am convinced it would have been a lot easier to start this method of including both our children, the day Nathan was diagnosed.

Everything we did and do to help Kate works somewhat. But then, how could it not? She is finally placed back at the center of our attention. She is getting what she always wanted, but now she comes at it from a different point of view than when she was younger. Now, she is more cynical and less open. She has confessed to me that she thinks everything that we do is to change her because we do not like her. She takes our actions to her or around her very personally. When we started addressing her anger issues, she needed constant attention and interactions because her self-esteem was very low. The best way to describe her was angry. SHE WAS ANGRY. Not at us per se, just angry.

As a family, we have tried several things to help mend our family bonds. We have seen counselors that are very helpful pointing out some of the things I discuss herein. Some lead us to change our environment, Kate's diet, or how to plan more things for her specifically. We spend a lot of time being clearer and more open about how we feel and what we expect of her. With her very large personality, not all of this worked, but we keep trying. We have learned there is no instant cure. This attitude of hers has developed over years of hurt, it can only be healed with even more years of understanding, effort and love.

I want to include here the two books that we received some of the best assistance with helping Kate know how much we love her:

Grace-Based Parenting – May 15, 2005, by Tim Kimmel (Author), Max Lucado (Foreword)

And

The Explosive Child: A New Approach for Understanding and Parenting Easily Frustrated, Chronically Inflexible Children – January 19, 2010, by Ross W., Ph.D. Greene (Author)

These books are based on the principle that there is no substitute for love, patience, understanding and trying to talk about things. Parents need to be involved and make sincere and extreme efforts to recover the relationship that may have been lost during the battle with cancer.

Over a year ago, Kate stopped going to a counselor. She is doing well and therapy was good but not helping as much anymore. We all had learned a new way to interact. I asked Kate if she wanted one more time with the counselor to talk about Nathan having cancer. She looked at me curiously. I explained that sometimes it is nice to talk to someone you trust just to say, "It was not fair." None of this was fair. She and I agreed that we could not prevent cancer. We agreed that we are working through it now and making great progress, but she deserved the opportunity to express her anger over the whole thing. To my surprise, she agreed and thought it was a great idea. She had her one last appointment to discuss anything she wanted. While I was not a participant in this meeting, her face was calmer and more peaceful when she finished.

One other thing we have learned through counseling is that we cannot go back and do things differently. Kate has her childhood memories, just like the rest of us do. Nathan getting cancer was not fair to anyone in the family. We all survived the battle even though we all have wounds from it. For example, I cannot go near any hospital without having a severe reaction and anxiety attack. Nathan has several physical ailments that will be with him forever, hearing loss, weak bones, etc. Scott made several Air Force career decisions that kept his family where they needed to be to care for Nathan no matter how it impacted his chance for advancement. We all have a little bit of baggage related to cancer. We all need to work together to help lighten this baggage across the entire family.

Figure 9 - Kate spending time on the beach with Mom January 1, 2013

Recently two events in our lives show how far we have come:

First, I started writing this book. I had completed the book Learning to Dance in the Rain: A Parent's Guide to Neuroblastoma Diagnosis, Treatment and Beyond in 2013. It chronicles our lives through pediatric oncology through Nathan's eyes. Over the next few years, I realized that Kate's story is just as important. I asked her first if I could write this book. She said yes. Then she agreed to be part of it. In several sections of this book, she has corrected me in things that I remember differently than she, or that she considers blatantly wrong. This book has given her an outlet. We are showing her how we feel, what we learned and what we will do to try to help other children avoid the same thing. Not only are we showing her how we feel, we are writing it down and showing anyone who wants to read this book.

Second, this past year Nathan had a spontaneous pneumothorax (collapsed lung). He went to the urgent care and then the Emergency Room (ER). I took Kate home while we were working through things because she really wanted to go home and sleep. It was late and she did not want to just sit in the ER watching her parents pace the floors while waiting for Nathan's treatment. We were suspicious that Nathan would need a chest tube. Kate and I both agreed that was going to be gross.

The next day we tried out the things I mention in this book. I dragged Kate to the hospital to sit with Nathan. We took board games, books and our electronics to pass the time. Luckily, things were very boring (with no new medical emergencies). We sat and talked, took short trips to the gift shop (this hospital does not have fish tanks) and basically watched Nathan sleep, breathe and be in pain. On the drive home from the hospital one of the four days, Kate looked at me very seriously and said "10 years! You have been doing this for 10 years?!" A little understanding coming through. The next day I gave her the option to stay home a few hours, or join me at the very boring hospital. No, she would not stay home, she was going where the action was. Granted, it was very slow, boring, sleepy, painful action, but it was her family doing it and that is where she was going to be. After four days with no new complications and a sealed inflated lung, Nathan came home.

Figure 10 - Kate having a little boat fun with Dad

I must admit at this point in Kate and my relationship I think we are getting along well. We each have our quirks that we bring to the dynamic, but we both know that we adore each other and are extremely happy to be in the same family. She even allows me to slightly redirect her negative attitudes when she is nervous and scared before an orchestra tryout, or the like.

Kate is Daddy's girl. She drags her father anywhere and everywhere. Her relationship with her brother is improving. She will never admit it directly to Nathan, but she has told me in confidence that she thinks Nathan is a pretty cool kid.

As I talk with Kate about writing this book, I have asked her what things she feels helped her the most to deal with Nathan's cancer. Her answer was "Morgan Le Fay," our dog "and you must put a picture of her in this book." When Morgan entered our house, she walked over, sat on Kate's small couch and claimed it and my daughter as her own. Best friends from that point on. I did not realize at the time how useful this dog would be for Kate's mental health, but I sure am glad she was around with us.

Figure 11 - Kate and Morgan Le Fay, one of her best friends

There is nothing in this world as important as our families. We get one time through our lives. Our children are worth all the effort and energy we can give them, no matter what our normal lives look like.

NOTES

_____

_____

_____

_____

_____

_____

_____

_____

_____

_____

_____

_____

_____

_____

NOTES

NOTES

CHAPTER 8. YOUR SPOUSE

The following is an excerpt from the book "…Learning to Dance in the Rain: A Parent's Guide to Neuroblastoma, Diagnosis, Treatment and Beyond"

Scott and I had been married for 14 years when Nathan was diagnosed with cancer. We had just taken our biggest vacation a month before it all began. We thought we were on firm ground as a couple to handle Nathan's diagnosis and treatment for neuroblastoma. We had our family and friends to help, we had our church and bible study groups to support us and we had an amazing medical staff to get us through it. And yet, the question I am asked the most frequently about this journey, is how did Scott and I stay together through it all. This is a tough journey on anyone. There are soul-wrenching days where you feel your child is not going to live through. There are harder days when you just do not want to go to the hospital to care for your child because it is just too hard. I do not think it is even possible to explain in words what a person goes through while watching their child being sick with cancer and going through such difficult treatments that may or may not cure them of their disease.

After the initial diagnosis, Scott and I clung to each other. He was my confidant; he was the only other person that understood what I was going through. He was going through it too. He was there every day, every moment, through everything. We had our talks in great depth about what to do and who should do it. We worked a rotating schedule with the children where we would alternate nights so we would each get to see Kate. We did not need to choose another treatment for months, so we were able just to support each other and work out whatever issues we had making day to day life somewhat normal. We had our journal to communicate and let each other know what we were feeling. We got into this autopilot mode of taking care of Nathan and not completely ignoring Kate. We were even able to, on occasion, get someone else to watch the children while we went to dinner and just chatted with each other. This is not a model that can be sustained for years, but it worked for us for months.

When we did have the opportunity to be together, whether at the hospital or elsewhere, we tried to reconnect as a couple and not let our circumstances completely get in the way. Sometimes this would be having a cup of coffee in the cafeteria while the kids were being cared for. Sometimes it was more playful. Sometimes, the boys (Nathan and Scott) would hide from me. When I got in range, both would jump out and pelt me with Nerf darts and laugh. Usually, we would sit quietly while Nathan slept and watch him while just being together. We were best friends. Anytime we could do something that was not cancer-related rejuvenated us as a couple.

Eventually, the stress took its toll. Nathan's treatments were not working as they should. Decisions had to be made by us that were potentially life threatening to Nathan. We were not sure what to do. We did not know how to release this helplessness and anger, so we took it out on each other. We yelled at each other out of pain for our child. We had screaming matches about which treatment options we should pick. One of them came after finishing a phone call with Nathan's doctor. I wanted to talk to Scott more about the treatment and just kept pestering him. In the end, we were yelling at each other not about anything specific but just because our plight looked so very hopeless.

After 3 years or so of harming our relationship and hurting each other, we did one thing right to mend and stopped a free fall to disaster. During a bible study exercise, we were to find something in our lives we could work on to improve. We chose to finally work on our marriage. It was time to stop taking from the relationship; now it was time to add to the relationship and daily. Sometimes it was something small like an intentional and loving kiss on the cheek, *"This is your one nice thing today. We are REALLY busy."* Sometimes it was bringing home our favorite dessert after a night of volleyball, feeding each other while resting on the couch. It did not matter really what it was, what mattered is that we were intentionally doing something to show the other one how much we loved them and they knew it. We continue to try to do this still today, but we do not always point them out. It sounds simple, *intentionally do one explicitly nice thing for your spouse daily*, but it sure does make a difference.

NOTES

NOTES

CHAPTER 9. NATHAN'S STORY

Photo was taken by Brendon Cox 2017

Nathan was diagnosed with stage IV Neuroblastoma on August 8, 2006. As mentioned in Kate's story, initially we were all in a panic. We met with doctors and got a plan in place. The first few months proceeded according to those plans. The surgeon was able to completely remove his primary tumor and put in his intravenous catheter. Chemotherapy started. He had two rounds of chemotherapy followed by his stem cells harvest. Four more rounds of varying chemotherapies as defined in the front-line therapy protocol. Treatments and side effects were just as predicted. He was able to work through several of the rarer side effects such as being allergic to a drug or two, getting an infection in his intravenous catheter, fighting sepsis, and other creative additions to an already difficult treatment plan.

All went as expected until we started preparing for Bone Marrow Transplant (BMT). We learned that Nathan did not have a lot of success in frontline therapy. The treatments did not work quite the way they were supposed to. Each treatment only worked to a certain degree. His body was still riddled with the disease in his bones. With the help of our medical team, we came up with one alternative treatment and then another.

When frontline therapy was over, Nathan's scans showed disease still riddled throughout his skeleton. His disease load was significantly lower than when he started but still too high to go into BMT. The worst possible scenario would be to go through BMT and still have active disease throughout his body. Then he would still have to fight but would have nothing to fight with because his immune system would be very weak. While researching treatments, we came across a different cocktail of chemotherapy which was not part of frontline therapy. He had a few rounds of it while we figured out what to do next. The new chemotherapy had the added benefit that it also reduced his disease load a bit more.

With the help of our two most trusted doctors, we came up with a new plan. There was a Phase II study that would include MIBG therapy just before BMT. It would be timed so that both treatments would have Nathan's blood counts going towards zero around the same time. This was a substantial risk for us. If the MIBG therapy did not reduce the disease load such that BMT could wipe out the remaining disease, we would once again be in the worst possible scenario. However, in our opinion and our doctors' opinions, this was Nathan's best chance to have a cure.

As with all of Nathan's treatments, it worked a bit but did not clear his disease. The first set of scans following BMT still showed disease throughout his skeleton and his bone marrow was still positive for neuroblastoma. He was supposed to do radiation next, but there was too much disease to radiate. The radiation oncologist made it clear he could not survive radiating all his remaining disease locations. It would be too toxic for his very weak body.

By this point in our journey, we had met and worked with many different doctors. We weighed pros and cons from each of their opinions. In the end, we kept coming back to two doctors. Their opinions and advice tended to work. We worked with them best. We trusted them and weighed their opinions higher than the rest. When at a cross road like just past BMT, we would find reasons to put ourselves in contact with these two doctors, in person. When you get that far off the primary treatment path, there are a lot of options out there and no one person knows which treatment is going to work. Each treatment option may or may not work on your child's cancer. Your child's cancer is different than another child's cancer. Each patient is unique.

With disease throughout Nathan's body and bone marrow after BMT and MIBG therapy, there were no more "big gun" therapies left. We were living out our worst-case scenario. We needed a completely new treatment plan. We needed something that was not as caustic as chemotherapy but would hold this disease off. We were presented with a few different options from the doctors. None of them sounded promising and all of them sounded like we were just giving up, except one. The one we chose was the riskiest. We were going to have Nathan go through another round of high dose chemotherapy and another stem cell rescue. Nathan would also have radiation therapy in specific worrisome areas instead of all the remaining disease since We were then going to go to another hospital for a Phase I antibody treatment. The treatment we had chosen was only available in one hospital. The biggest concern was whether Nathan was strong enough to get through another high dose chemotherapy right after finishing BMT. We felt that he could survive this and it was truly our only option. We believed if we did not do this treatment at this point we would lose this option. We needed to choose this now, or never choose it.

We had one big decision left and that was where to do the high-risk chemotherapy and radiation. Do we do it at our home hospital where the doctor completely agrees with the treatment plan? Life would be easier for us and we would get to see Kate, but we would need to travel twice a day 45 minutes away for radiation. Or, do we do it at the BMT hospital where the doctor did not necessarily agree with our treatment option? It would probably be the safest place to have it done, but we would be away from home another month and we were ready to no longer be in that hospital. Not only that, how do you even proceed to get a treatment plan in place specified by doctors that are states away? What paperwork would we need and how long would it take to implement it? Who would coordinate all the different types of treatment? Who would be in charge when the doctor dictating the treatment was not even in this hospital? Who would deal with insurance?

I arrived at one of Nathan's post BMT meetings to ask some of these questions and tell the doctor that our decision was to do the treatment at our home hospital (not the BMT hospital). We wanted some normalcy and to see Kate. Before I could finalize this decision, the doctor told me the answer to all the above questions. I was informed how many documents would need to be done and who would need to sign them. I was told of all the dangers and the coordinating issues. I was told of issues I had not thought about. There were now, even more, things to resolve than before. Then the doctor handed me all the signed documents I would need for the treatment to be done at the BMT hospital. The plan was already in place and all I had to do was agree to it, so, I did. It was an excellent choice on our part. The very first evening of Nathan's high dose chemotherapy he spiked a 104F fever. He stayed in the hospital for four weeks.

Treatment went according to plan. Nathan had high dose chemotherapy followed by a stem cell rescue. He then had radiation treatments twice a day for ten days. He enjoyed these because he got to take an ambulance to the radiation center two times a day. Once all chemotherapy and radiation were completed, we traveled to yet another hospital for his antibody therapy. He ended up having four rounds of antibody therapy before beginning to have enough negative reactions (toxicities) to the treatment that it had to be stopped.

After six months, this new treatment plan was done. Once again, the treatment worked a bit but did not cure Nathan of cancer. Antibody therapy was states away from home and very tough. We were all exhausted physically and mentally and we still had this horrible disease throughout Nathan's body. It was smaller, but it was still there and Nathan's bone marrow was still positive for neuroblastoma.

We were then back asking questions and back to research treatments on the Internet. The one thing we did have this time was that Nathan was a bit stronger; he was almost a year past BMT. But it was time to find something other than chemotherapy for him. We had been poisoning him for almost 2 years and it just was not killing cancer cells. We had tried all the proven treatments and he was not clear of disease. We were now entering the area of experimental medicine. No one knew which therapies would work and which therapies would not work. We were down to the very last options available for Nathan. In the end, we came to two choices. There were two Phase II studies that looked a little more promising than taking Nathan off all treatment completely. We were fortunate enough to meet the lead doctor of one of the studies at a parent neuroblastoma conference. He informed us that in his opinion his study was not far enough along for Nathan. He recommended we try the other Phase II study first and, when we were done with that, hopefully, his study would be ready for us. So, that is what we did.

Nathan started his Phase II study in August of 2008. The drug was designed to keep Nathan's disease stable. It was not designed to kill the neuroblastoma, just keep it from growing too quickly. We expected Nathan to be able to take this drug for at least eight rounds. At least we hoped for eight rounds. That would give us six months to decide what to do next, not that there were many options left.

The next six months went very slowly. Every ache, every pain, every twitch, every complaint from Nathan immediately made us think that he was progressing and our fight was over. However, those eight rounds came and went and Nathan continued to be stable. Then, another eight rounds came and went and still stable. After 2 years of this treatment, the drug company completed the study. The drug had completely failed. Of the 95 or so children on the drug, it had helped one. Nathan was the only documented case we heard of responding to this drug at all. Not only did it keep Nathan's disease stable, it cleared many tumor beds. We were going to keep him on this drug as long as we could.

Soon there was a new problem. We had a drug that worked on Nathan, but the study was ending. The staff at our hospital worked with the drug manufacturer and the FDA to get a compassionate use waiver for Nathan. They effectively created a study for one person, Nathan. He was going to be able to continue this drug until the company stopped making it. That gave us three more years on the drug, which brought us to February 2015.

Once again, the drug was taken off the market. It continued to fail all its medical trials. Nathan was also showing significant side effects from the drug. His peripheral neuropathy had reached a level that he could no longer ignore. His pain was significant when he walked. We were considering stopping the drug due to does limiting toxicity when it went off the market. In February 2015, Nathan stopped taking his experimental drug or any other treatment for Neuroblastoma.

Before we were willing to completely remove Nathan from all treatment we needed to evaluate our options. We consulted Neuroblastoma experts. They gave us a few options.

➢ We could stop all treatment and watch what happens.
➢ We could put him back on chemotherapy, but we did not know what we were even fighting.
➢ We could try to take a bone biopsy at the site in his tibia that was still MIBG positive. With a piece of tissue, we would be more educated to evaluate all treatment options.

The disease positive area in his right tibia was the brightest spot on the MIBG scan. The plan was to perform a CT scan on his tibia to find the "holes" in his bones where the disease was residing. Then we would perform an MRI on the same location to find a piece of tissue we would remove with a needle biopsy. And finally, a CT guided needle biopsy to take sample of tissue to evaluate for neuroblastoma.

The CT scan showed no holes in his bones. They had all healed. The MRI showed no tissue in the tibia to evaluate. There was no need for the biopsy because the disease was gone. On May 27, 2015, Nathan was declared NED, No Evidence of Disease.

A year later in May 2016, Nathan had another set of MIBG scans. Nathan is considered "cured" and entered the survivorship program!!!

The family now has a new outlook on life, hospitals and our future. We are now focused on minimizing all forms or radiation and treatment. Nathan's body and mind need to learn how to grow and be normal. The dentist assistants look at us funny when we no longer allow dental x-rays. He has pulled through the worst of the worst and now it is our job to keep diligent in his care and education.

His story does not end with just his aches and pains. His story continues as he enters High School. Nathan has pushed beyond any of the boundaries set for him. He was told that he would never walk correctly or be able to run because of the Avascular Necrosis in his right hip. Nathan is a 2nd degree black belt in Taekwondo. He is a tuba player in his high school marching band, loves to play volleyball and has hiked the high adventure course in Philmont New Mexico. Nathan was told that school will always be a struggle and he needed to make realistic goals with respect to school. Nathan with the help of his school system is now a straight A honor student. He joined the middle schools Science Olympiad team where he placed 3rd in the state in the category of Microbe Missions. I must correct something. Nathan's parents were told these things about Nathan. He was never allowed to dwell in the negative impossibilities according to the doctors. He has decided what he wants to do and we help him get there as we can. To this point, Nathan is leading his own life as he sees fit. Yes, he deals with hearing loss, pain, lungs that are now working quite right and several other side effects, but he has chosen to excel regardless.

NOTES

_____

_____

_____

_____

_____

NOTES

CHAPTER 10. ORGANIZATIONS AND RESOURCES

Below are organizations we have had the pleasure to work with. There are many resources out there; please make use of them.

Children's Neuroblastoma Cancer Foundation (CNCF)

CNCF is an organization of parents of children with neuroblastoma. Their purpose is to educate other parents about this disease and then to fund research to cure it. I have been told that parents of neuroblastoma patients are a tight knit group and this organization is one of the reasons why. CNCF holds a parent conference each year where families and doctors come together to discuss the issues of neuroblastoma and how to solve them. Their website has a "Parent Handbook" that gives detailed information on everything you need to know about neuroblastoma. If you need help with anything, you can contact this organization directly.

Children's Neuroblastoma Cancer Foundation (CNCF)
360 W. Schick Rd., Suite 23 #211
Bloomingdale, IL 60108

Phone: (866) 671-2623
Fax: (630) 351-2462
Email: info@cncfhope.org
Website: http://www.cncfhope.org

Hospital Social Workers

Each hospital has a group of social workers available for the families. These people can help find the resources needed by a family, whether it is financial or something else. If you need anything outside of medical care at the hospital, ask for the social worker assigned to you.

Ronald McDonald House

The Ronald McDonald House is an organization with "houses" near hospitals. These Houses are available for families to stay in while caring for a sick child. The cost is minimal or free if money is an issue. Many local organizations bring in food and gifts for the children. It is a great option when getting treatment away from home or a good place to stay after bone marrow transplant or other long duration treatments. We stayed at two different Ronald McDonald Houses during our journey. One of them was for cancer patients only. We cannot say enough wonderful things about this organization.

Ronald McDonald House Charities
One Kroc Drive
Oak Brook, IL 60523

Phone: (630) 623-7048
Fax: (630) 623-7488
Email: info@rmhc.org

Candlelighters

Candlelighters is an organization of parents at the local hospital level. This organization helped us with information and care at the hospital in which Nathan was diagnosed. They supported us with books they published to help with some of the major family concerns, for example, other children dealing with a sibling with cancer, how to let the patient attend school, etc. Also, the families that were in Candlelighters had a lot of local information on resources available at that hospital. Not all hospitals have a Candlelighters organization, so check where you are.

Corporate Angel Network

Corporate Angel Network is an organization that works with corporations that have commuter jets that fly regularly scheduled commuter flights. The corporation allows patients and their families fly on these jets for treatment. We could fly on The Limited's corporate jet many times to take Nathan to his antibody therapy. There was no cost to us and the crew on the airplane welcomed us with open arms. Nathan could visit the cockpit most flights.

Corporate Angel Network, Inc.
Westchester County Airport
One Loop Road
White Plains, NY 10604-1215

Phone: (914) 328-1313
Toll-Free: (866) 328-1313
Fax: (914) 328-3938
Email: info@corpangelnetwork.org
Website: http://www.corpangelnetwork.org/

Project Angel Hugs

There are a few organizations out there just to make your child feel better just for a bit. Project Angel Hugs sends hugs to your child through the mail. These hugs come in the form of letters from other kids, cards, post cards and packages of gifts. They are very thoughtful around most holidays and they send a package of toys and gifts for your child. They even include presents for your other children, too. Nathan and Kate both squeal whenever they see an Angel Hugs box arrive in the mail. What a glorious few moments as they open it.

Project Angel Hugs
307 E. Mill Street, Suite 1
Plymouth, WI 53073
Phone: (920) 892-9138
Fax: (757) 873-8999
Website: http://www.projectangelhugs.com

Special Wish Foundation

Special Wish Foundation is one of the many organizations that fulfill the wish of a sick child. The wish can vary from a trip to Disney (like we took) to a play room (for a friend of ours) to a new computer for school. It just depends on the wish of the child and the ability of the organization to complete it.

A Special Wish Foundation, Inc.
National Headquarters
1250 Memory Lane N - Suite B
Columbus, Ohio 43209

Phone: (614) 258-3186
Toll-Free: (800) 486-wish
Fax: (614) 258-3518
Website: http://www.spwish.org/

Give Kids the World (GKTW)

Give Kids the World village is a resort in Orlando for sick children. GKTW works with the children "Wish" organizations to give children a week in the village. Its mission is to fulfill children's wishes and let them play like a child for a week. The village itself has enough things to do to keep anyone busy for a week. In addition, they have tickets available for Disney, Sea World, water parks, alligator farms, air boat rides, etc. After you have been to GKTW for a wish trip, anytime you are in Orlando, you are welcome to go visit for the day. You can use their facilities, have a meal and play. We have been back once since our Wish trip.

Give Kids The World Village
210 South Bass Road
Kissimmee, FL 34746

Phone: (407) 396-1114
Toll-Free: (800) 995-KIDS
Fax: (407) 396-1207
Website: http://www.gktw.org/

NOTES

NOTES

NOTES

NOTES

CHAPTER 11. FINAL COMMENTS

We are forever changed by our journey through childhood cancer. We are all better people. We are truly blessed as a family. We have been through this horrid disease and we still have our son and our daughter. We noticed how our family and daughter were slipping away early enough that we were able to make the correct changes to save it. Kate has received the love, attention and medical care she needed. Scott and I have refocused our energy into having a loving Christian marriage that is the center of our lives with our faith. We have learned how to tell both of our children how much they mean to us and why we do the things we do. It is my hope that the words in this book will help other families find that child that is somewhat forgotten in the total chaos of a long-term illness in the family. Each child in the family is precious and deserve our love and attention. Sometimes we just need to be reminded of that.

Rachel Ormsby is a wife, mother of two, aerospace engineer and has earned her second Dan (black belt) in Taekwondo with her son Nathan and a budding Ukulele player. When not running a household, she develops science hardware for the space program. This has included experiments on the Space Shuttle looking for new treatments for cancer, a cure for deafness and innovative ways to treat bone disease. Most recently she has worked on a bone densitometer for the International Space Station. She is the author of many scientific publications and co-holder of a patent. Rachel is the mother of Nathan and Kate. She is also the author of "...Learning to Dance in the Rain: A Parent's Guide to Neuroblastoma Diagnosis, Treatment and Beyond." Nathan was diagnosed with Stage IV Neuroblastoma in August of 2006 when he was three and Kate was 1-year-old. When Nathan was diagnosed, Rachel extended a planned "maternity leave" from her engineering career by an additional 7 years to care for Nathan and Kate. She has been married to her husband, Scott, since 1992.

Rev. Mamie Johnson founded MJ MINISTRIES INC. in January 2010. Growing up in inner city Cleveland, Ohio she understands the importance of having the proper support and guidance when faced with difficulty. It is through the selfless acts of others that a people and the world can be changed.

Rev. Johnson is a licensed and ordained minister of the gospel and holds a Bachelor of Science degree in Business Management from the University of Phoenix and a Master of Arts degree in Theology from Xavier University in Cincinnati, Ohio. Along with serving as the President of MJ Ministries Inc., she is an author, "When God Doesn't Stop the Rain (an autobiographical account of the many adversities she faced)" and Every Day the Master Speaks (a 365-day daily devotional) available at www.amazon.com). Rev. Johnson is a chaplain, a teacher, a Pastor, a facilitator and a dynamic conference speaker.

Rev. Johnson can be contacted by email at
www.mamiejohnson.com.

MJ Ministries, Inc.| P.O. Box 498999 | Cincinnati, OH 45249
MJ Ministries, Incorporated © 2010
mjministriesinc@gmail.com
MJ Ministries Inc. is a qualified IRS Section 501(c) (3) Organization

Figure 12 - The original photo used for the cover page of this book.
Kate at Disney during our Special Wish Foundation trip.